WHEN MICHAELS MET THE UNUSUAL

THE PERFECT COUPLE

James Marsh Sternberg MD (Dr J)

authorHOUSE®

AuthorHouse™
1663 Liberty Drive
Bloomington, IN 47403
www.authorhouse.com
Phone: 833-262-8899

Published by AuthorHouse 01/27/2022

ISBN: 978-1-6655-5054-3 (sc)
ISBN: 978-1-6655-5053-6 (e)

Print information available on the last page.

Also by James Marsh Sternberg

Playing to Trick One; No Mulligans in Bridge

Trump Suit Headaches; Rx for Declarers

The Finesse; Only a Last Resort

Blocking and Unblocking

Shortness – A Key to Better Bidding

When Michaels Met The Unusual

From Zero to Three Hundred

With Danny Kleinman

Second Hand High; Third Hand Not So High

An Entry, An Entry; My Kingdom For an Entry

L O L: It's Loser on Loser

In Search of a Second Suit

Elimination and Endplays

DEDICATION

To Dr. Stephen Schulman

My career-long radiology partner
who made it fun to come to
work and made my life easier.

Thanks for all the good times, pard.

ACKNOWLEDGMENTS

This book would not have been possible without the help of several friends. Frank Stewart, Michael Lawrence, Anne Lund, Eddie Kantar, Danny Kleinman, and Marty Bergen all provided suggestions for material for the book.

I am forever indebted to Hall of Famer Fred Hamilton and both the late Bernie Chazen and Allan Cokin, without whose guidance and teaching I could not have achieved whatever success I have had in bridge.

Many thanks to my editor, Paul Linxwiler, who only makes my writing better than it really is.

And, of course, Vickie Lee Bader, whose love and patience helped guide me through the many hours of this endeavor.

James Marsh Sternberg, MD
Palm Beach Gardens FL
mmay001@aol.com

CONTENTS

INTRODUCTION

Two-Suited Overcalls: The Whole Story

Life Before Michaels or Anybody Else

In the early days of bridge, a direct cue bid of your right hand opponent's opening bid was traditionally played as a "strong" cue bid, a hand too powerful for an ordinary take-out double, forcing to game. A typical hand was any 4–4–4–1 hand with 18–19+ HCP.

These occurred so seldom players found they could start with a take-out double, so the direct cue bid was finally put to better use. The most popular use is to show some form of a two-suited hand.

The Michaels Cue Bid is one of the most popular conventions among players in the United States. Say you're in second seat and you have a nice hand. You have only 11 HCP, but nice distribution: 1=5=1=6. And of course, you are going to open your long suit first. But hey, wait a minute. Your RHO is pulling something out of his bidding box. That's not fair. This isn't going to be so easy.

But we have lots of tools to describe two-suited hands. The two most popular are the Michaels Cue Bid and the Unusual Notrump. The parameters for both conventions are the same. To start, one should have at least 5–5 distribution. Some partnerships restrict their use of both conventions for hands that are either "weak" or "strong" but not in the "middle" range. This idea, however, has been losing favor with most expert partnerships who rightly feel shape trumps strength.

The more modern view is that the distributional nature of their hand outweighs any disadvantage. They prefer entering the auction as soon as possible regardless of strength. That can be worried about later in the auction. We will discuss this in more detail in later chapters.

What we have is a way of putting to use bids that are rarely needed in a natural sense in order to describe shapely hands that would be otherwise awkward to bid. In the past, a 2NT overcall showed a balanced hand of 20–22 HCP, which occurs infrequently after the opponents have opened the bidding. But if you do have such a powerhouse, you can start with double. Similarly, overcalling the opponent's suit, (e.g., 1♢–2♢) was used to show a hand too strong for a take-out double, a real monster, insisting on game. Again, starting with double works fine.

So it became logical to put these bids to better use. After all, when the opponents bid first, it can be difficult to compete effectively, to be able to get both suits into the auction before the level gets too high. These hands often have tremendous trick-taking potential due to their distributional value if partner holds a fit for one or both of your suits.

These bids can be both constructive and destructive. And often, very early in the auction, the overcaller does not know for sure which. He may have a strong hand or a weak hand. Subsequent bidding will reveal which, but his partner should assume weak on the first round of bidding.

How much strength does the overcaller need? There are many factors, and we will look at all of them. As expert player and author Jerry Helms is often quoted, "Look for a reason to bid, not an excuse to pass."

Most of the deals presented will show your hand at the top of the page with a partial auction given. Try to answer the questions posed and decide what to bid before looking at the whole deal that follows.

CHAPTER 1
Kissing Cousins

KISSING COUSINS

Why are Michaels and the Unusual Notrump conventions linked together? Because they have so much in common, they must be related like cousins. Let's see what they have in common and how they differ. Neither is Alertable in ACBL-sanctioned events.

They are both conventional bids to show two-suited hands, not necessarily of great strength. Both are based more on distribution, and the strength is closely tied to the vulnerability of the particular deal. The advantage of the overcaller being able to show both his suits with a weak hand with relative safety makes these tools extremely useful.

The Michaels Cue Bid is more focused on the majors while the Unusual Notrump focuses on the minors. There is some variation in the latter as we will see.

In both, the partner of the overcaller, called the "advancer," bases his responses more on fits with the overcaller, and the number of tricks he thinks his side (and the opponents' side) might take. The strategy is similar to how you would think after partner opened a two- or three-level bid.

These bids can be used in both a constructive and/or a destructive fashion, based on degrees of fits, strength, and vulnerability. It is important to develop judgment in using these tools, in responding to these bids, and also how to handle competition when the opponents are using these conventions against you.

TWO-SUITED OVERCALLS: LET ME COUNT THE WAYS

There are various ways of showing a two-suited hand. Everybody has their favorites. "If you don't like mine, yours is no good," is often heard. Many players assume there is only one way to play, their own method, and complain loudly when anyone disagrees.

The best known are Michaels, coupled with the Unusual Notrump and Ghestem. For completeness, here is a list of some of the others:

Schroeder

Michaels

Bailey or Modified Michaels

Quantum or Modified Wenble

CRO

Ghestem

Ghestem per Blue Club

Wenble or Ghestem

Roman Jumps

CRO is Color, Rank, and Other. An alternative is CRASH, meaning the third bid shows two suits of the same SHAPE.

Many players play the Unusual Notrump alone, but Ghestem and Michaels incorporate Unusual Notrumps.

Quantum was named for "Cue Bid, Unusual, and Michaels" by Mr. Wenble.

Colorful Cue Bids, by Dorothy Truscott, show unbid suits of the same color.

Top & Bottom Cue Bids show the highest- and lowest-ranking unbid suits.

Some play a jump cue bid to show the same suits as a single cue bid would, but with greater distribution and/or strength.

CHAPTER 2

When To Make A Two-Suited Overcall

WHEN TO MAKE A TWO-SUITED OVERCALL

Regardless of which conventional system your partnership has chosen, the first question is when to make an overcall with a two-suited hand. What are the factors to consider? First. some general thoughts.

Shape Requirements: I strongly urge you to not to show a two-suiter in the direct seat unless your pattern is 5–5 or better. Being adventurous with 5–4 patterns will only discourage your partner, who will "always" bid your four-card suit and play in a tenuous 4–3 fit. (Mike Michaels' original requirement was 4–4: scary.)

Strength Requirements: In the past, some authorities advocated showing two-suited hands conventionally only with a weak hand or a very strong hand. This, I believe, is misguided. Why? Well, for one thing, if opener has 12–15 HCP and the overcaller (you) have 13–15 HCP, your 1♠ overcall could certainly end the bidding. Very nice: Playing and struggling to make 1♠ in your 5–2 fit, while you're cold for 4♡ in your 4–5 fit.

When opener has a two-suited hand, it's relatively easy to show the two suits separately and with natural bidding. Overcaller rarely has that opportunity. Overcaller risks getting passed out or getting preempted and the second suit is still sitting there.

In fact, of the three hand types (weak, opening-bid values, and very strong), if you want to exclude one from Michaels, you should exclude the strong one. Usually that player has no problem bidding twice or starting with an off-shape take-out double.

The first criterion was suit length. With few exceptions, a minimum of 5–5 distribution is a starting point. Your partner is going to base his response on how well the hands fit, on how many cards he has in one of your suits. If you constantly table a dummy with a four-card suit and start mumbling something about whatever, your partner will remember. And when the same scenario occurs, your partner may be reluctant to make the right bid, fearing you again are 4–5 in the two suits.

There are exceptions. Expert player and author Marty Bergen showed a hand that he said that at favorable vulnerability, he would show the majors with two very attractive suits: ♠ K Q J 10 ♡ Q J 10 9 8 ◇ 2 ♣ 4 3 2.

This is the exception, not the rule.

What about the strength of your hand? It makes no sense to say one needs X number of high-card points. I saw a pair once agree they needed 8 HCP to bid Michaels and did so with: ♠ 8 6 4 3 2 ♡ Q 9 7 5 3 ◇ Q J ♣ K.

But the same player later passed with: ♠ Q J 8 6 5 4 ♡ K J 10 8 7 ◇ 10 ♣ 8, explaining to her partner that she only had 7 HCP. This "point counter" needs to take up a different game.

The importance of the intermediate spot cards cannot be overemphasized. You rarely hear a penalty double when you, not the opponents, have the intermediates. As Bergen said, "All two-suiters are not created equal."

Suit quality may vary depending on vulnerability. What looks satisfactory at one vulnerability may be completely unacceptable at another. On his website, expert player and author Larry Cohen uses the example of ♠ Q 9 8 7 5 ♡ K J 8 4 2 as being just fine at favorable for a Michael's bid, but with the same suits at unfavorable vulnerability, Cohen says "it wouldn't occur to me to commit a Michaels bid over 1♣ with the same holding."

Like preempting, the vulnerability is important. This is where suit quality may be the most important. Just because you are vulnerable should not deter you from bidding, but suit quality and having your points in your suits are factors to consider. And if partner is a passed hand, that adds a touch of caution too.

The level of the bidding is very important. Consider the difference between how much space your partner has after 1♣–2♣ compared to 1♠–2♠, whatever system you are playing. So not all suits are created equal either.

What's the upper limit of high-card values for a Michaels Cue Bid? In the past, these bids were played as "weak," 8–11 HCP, or strong, 16+. If you had a hand with 12–15 HCP, the idea was to bid your higher-ranked suit first and then hope to bid your other suit. That was fine in the past before players started to learn to bid and preempt on fewer values.

I recently read an article on Michaels where in the center, in capital letters, it said, "DO NOT USE WITH INTERMEDIATE HANDS (12–14)." Few experienced partnerships play that way anymore. Expert and prolific author Mike Lawrence recently pointed out in an article that over the years it has become acceptable to have almost any range for this bid. Why?

The problem is in the old days, it was common for the bidding to proceed as follows: 1♣–1♠(you)–2♣–Pass; Pass. You could bid your other suit, perhaps 2♡. Nowadays, it likely comes back to you at 4♣. Great! Now what? Are you bidding 4♡? I don't think so. But if you had bid 2♣ over 1♣, you wouldn't be in this mess. Shape trumps points.

While there is still some difference of opinion on this, I certainly go along with Lawrence. Bergen says, "When you can show both majors in one bid, that's a good thing to do." If it's good enough for these guys, I'm in.

As with any convention, you need to make sure if it is "on" in the following situations:

By a passed hand? Most recommend YES.

In the balancing seat? Most recommend YES.

After opponents bid 1 anything–Pass–1NT? Most recommend YES.

After the opponents bid and raise, e.g., 1♡–Pass–2♡? Needs to be discussed.

After weak two-bids, e.g., 2♡–3♡? Most recommend NO.

What are some of the factors which will influence your decision and help answer the question, "Should I make a two-suited overcall?" Here is a list which may help in your decision:

Suit length: In direct seat, a minimum of 5–5 shape is strongly suggested.

Strength of your hand: Varies with the other factors, much more on this later.

Vulnerability: Obviously a lot of leeway at favorable, more caution otherwise.

Level of the bidding: Usually the two level.

Suit quality: Intermediates are really important.

Obstructive value: Do you have a good hand? Whose hand might it be?

Opponents' skill: Who's pushing who around?

Holding in opponent's suits: Are your honor cards working or in your short suits?

Opponents' methods: How well can they handle your obnoxious interference?

GENERAL THOUGHTS FOR RESPONDER

After your partner has made a two-suited overcall, what should you be thinking about? The answer is the same to either Michaels or the Unusual Notrump. You need ask yourself some questions.

First and foremost, do I have a fit in one or more of the suits my partner has shown? If yes, great! If not, hope your RHO bids and gets you off the hook. If you have a fit, how good is the fit? How many trumps do you have? Three is nice, but four is huge!

How many tricks do you think your side might take? Do you have any "cover" cards? Partner has three outside cards: Do you have any aces to cover these losers? Kings and queens in those outside suits are probably of no value.

Do you think the opponents can make something, assuming partner does not have the infrequent "big" two-suiter? What is the vulnerability? Is -300 or -500 going to be a good score? If they can make a slam, even -800 would be a good score (if they bid and make it).

The advancer should be less concerned about counting his high-card points. Tricks, trump fits and cover cards are far more important. When advancer bids, he is not so much thinking about what he can make, but should be thinking about how to try to optimize his result by keeping the opponents from reaching their best result.

If responder thinks he has enough of a fit and enough tricks, he should bid game. With nine or ten trumps, bid game and hope to make it. If you go down, you have probably preempted the opponents out of their best contract anyhow.

On the other hand, if you do NOT have a fit, staying as low as possible is crucial.

CHAPTER 3
The Michaels Cue Bid

THE MICHAELS CUE BID

The Michaels Cue Bid was invented by the late Michael Michaels of Miami Beach, FL. He was a friend and frequent partner of Charles Goren, for whom he ghostwrote the popular column in the newspapers. Michaels died at an early age from throat cancer.

Michaels Cue Bids are defined as follows:

(1♣)–2♣ = the majors
(1♢)–2♢ = the majors
(1♡)–2♡ = spades and an unspecified minor
(1♠)–2♠ = hearts and an unspecified minor

Let's look at some typical hands starting with the majors after the opponents open a minor. A typical hand should be 5–5 in the majors with a minimum of 8 HCP in your two suits.

♠A Q 6 4 2 ♡K 10 9 8 4 ♢5 ♣5 3 would be fine at equal or favorable vulnerability. At unfavorable, you would like a better spade suit, perhaps ♠A Q 10 9 8. Suit quality is important, more so than an extra point or two.

♠K Q 9 7 3 ♡A J 10 9 4 ♢J 4 ♣8 or ♠A Q 9 7 3 ♡K Q 10 9 5 ♢4 ♣7 3 would both be satisfactory.

♠A Q 9 5 3 ♡K J 5 4 3 ♢4 ♣A 3 is an opening hand which modern players would bid Michaels with, while others would prefer overcalling 1♠.
I, of course, would bid Michaels.

♠A Q J 6 4 ♡A K 10 6 5 ♢5 3 ♣2, a hand from an article years ago which said "unsuitable for Michaels, bid 1♠." I can't imagine not bidding Michaels.
A 1♠ overcall might be the end of the auction. Bye-bye hearts.

♠A 9 7 3 2 ♡J 10 6 5 4 ♢5 ♣7 6. Weak, yes, but at favorable vulnerability, is a fine hand for Michaels. Pass otherwisc.

And when they open a major, a Michaels Cue Bid shows 5–5 in the other major and an unspecified minor. If you are 5–6, with six of the minor, even better. If you are 6–5 with six of the major, it's usually best to try to overcall the major.

Of course, this is not always possible. A two-over-one overcall should show a good hand.

Some examples of typical Michaels hands after a 1♡ opening:

♠ A Q 9 6 4 ♡ 4 ◇ A J 9 6 3 ♣ 7 3. This is acceptable.

Are hearts and spades equal? Not quite. After an auction (1♡)–2♡, partner might be able to bid at the two level, which is not possible after (1♠)–2♠. So you might need just a bit more for the latter auction.

That's it. Overcalling with a Michaels Cue Bid is relatively easy. It does require some judgment, but there's a lot a latitude. Partnerships should discuss and agree on the parameters.

What requires more discussion and judgment is how to continue after partner has made a two-suited overcall. Let's take a look in the next few pages.

RESPONDING TO MICHAELS

Because the Michaels Cue Bid is a common convention, we need to consider how to respond after partner uses it. The advancer is going to initially assume overcaller has the weaker hand and bid accordingly.

Let's first assume the next player passes. After (1 minor)–2 minor, if advancer bids 2♡/2♠, he denies any interest in going on. He might be bidding a two-card suit. Remember, your bid was forcing. What was he supposed to do with a hand with 2=2=4=5 distribution? Even a hand like ♠ 6 5 ♡ 9 5 2 ◇ K J 7 4 ♣ A J 8 5 isn't worth more than a 2♡ response. Sure, you have values, but they are all opposite partner's shortness. Don't even think about 2NT.

A hand such as: ♠ Q 2 ♡ J 9 8 ◇ K J 5 4 2 ♣ K Q 4 has 12 HCP and three hearts. How high would you bid? How much is this hand really worth?

Let's give partner a typical Michaels hand and see:

You	Partner
♠Q 2	♠K 9 6 5 4
♡J 9 8	♡A Q 9 8 7
◇K J 5 4 2	◇9
♣K Q 4	♣8 7

On this layout, you are missing three aces. By the time you set up the spades, you have to lose at least one. If hearts are 4–1 and spades 4–2, even a 2♡ contract might be too high.

So what have we seen? The number of trumps is key. Two is really bad. Three is nice but consider the other factors. Four, however, is great! Also shape beats high-card points. And your HCP need to be working.

Any jump raise in partner's known suit is preemptive, bidding to the level of the fit (eight trumps = two level, nine trumps = three level, etc.). A jump raise shows good support rather than points, an example of "support with support." Putting maximum pressure on the opponents is more important than worrying about if you are going to be able to make what you bid.

If overcaller has shown a major-minor two-suiter, many pairs often play that 2NT asks for the minor. But 2NT can be better used as a game try in the major. Consider the auction of (1♠)–2♠. Advancer's only choice in hearts is to sign off in 3♡ or bid game. Not much room, but if she can make a game try with 2NT, a more accurate contract may be reached. Notice after (1♡)–2♡, there is more room for exploring spade contracts.

To find partner's minor, responder can simply bid 3♣, asking overcaller to pass or correct to 3◇. With a stronger interest in the minor, advancer can bypass by bidding 3◇ initially. This differs from what might be considered standard, and needs to be discussed. But, hey, that's why you bought this book, to learn some newer bidding tools.

The above is a simple explanation. In real life, often the opposition is bidding.

A common-sense approach is required. These situations require a good understanding of general principles rather than trying to memorize responses.

We will look at many examples.

After (1♣)–2♣, showing the majors:

♠5 4 ♡K Q 10 5 ◇10 6 4 ♣J 7 5 3
Regardless of the vulnerability, with excellent support, bid 3♡.

♠9 6 ♡A 8 6 4 2 ◇8 6 4 2 ♣A 5
With this hand, you don't need much to make game. Bid 4♡.

♠5 3 ♡K 8 ◇8 6 4 ♣A J 10 9 8 6
Take a simple preference to 2♡. Do NOT pass partner's forcing bid. She might have a huge hand.

♠5 3 ♡K 8 ◇A J 10 9 8 6 ♣8 6 4
Same hand as above with the minors reversed, but you can bid 2◇. Partner can still bid if she likes.

♠8 6 4 ♡Q 4 ◇K Q 10 5 ♣K Q J 4
Your HCP are not working. Bid 2♠.

Bergen suggests using 2NT as a game try after this sequence, with these responses:

3♣ = minimum, equal or better hearts

3♢ = minimum, better spades

3♡ = non-minimum, equal or better hearts

3♠ = non-minimum, better spades

With a hand such as: ♠ K 6 3 ♡ K 6 ♢ 9 7 4 ♣ A 6 5 4 3, you could bid 2NT.

Lawrence suggests using 2NT as a game try with these responses:

3♣ = minimum with longer hearts

3♢ = minimum with longer spades

3♡ = minimum with 5–5 in the majors

3♠ = maximum with longer hearts

3NT = maximum with longer spades

4♣ = maximum, equal length, club shortness

4♢ = maximum, equal length, diamond shortness

Lawrence writes "There's some memory work involved, but don't knock it until you've tried it!"

After (1 major)–2 major, showing the other major and an unspecified minor:

How should advancer bid? If he has a major-suit fit, a decision must be made regarding level. With a weak hand, advancer should think about preempting. But what if he is interested in game? What choice do you have over (1♠)–2♠? It's 3♡ to play or 4♡, and you are in game. Not a lot of choices. It's a little easier after (1♡)–2♡, but still, it's challenging.

So if you play that 2NT asks for partner's minor, the way many of us first learned, how can you make a major-suit game try? So let's stop doing that. 2NT should say instead, "I'm interested in game in your major," and 3♣ is pass or correct.

Constructive game tries after a Michaels showing a major and a minor

Using 2NT as "I'm interested in a game in your major," how should overcaller respond? Sometimes advancer's decision to continue might hinge on knowing which minor overcaller has, but advancer can't ask playing this method. However, expert Danny Kleinman (my frequent co-author) suggests that to have it both ways in responding to a 2NT inquiry, overcaller bid his major with extras, his minor with a minimum. Then advancer can make an informed decision. He knows both the minor and if opener has extra values.

Fourth Seat Michaels

Another hearts-versus-spades problem arises in the fourth seat. Say the auction starts 1 Major–Pass–2 Major–Michaels (or 2NT Unusual). When their suit is hearts, you can stop in 3♠. But if their suit is spades, your 3♠ Michaels bid forces you into 4♡.

Another Kleinman suggestion is Inverting Fourth Seat Michaels. Use 2NT as Michaels to allow stopping in 3♡ and use 3♠ for the minors. While it's more important in spades, for purposes of memory, it's best to use for both suits. Therefore, 1 Major–Pass–2 Major–2NT = Michaels, but 1 Major–Pass–2 Major–3 Their Major = Unusual for minors.

Responding to Michaels after RHO Intervenes

Let's consider some of our options when your RHO takes some action other than pass when your partner has bid Michaels.

RHO Doubles. The double can mean various things. Should you ask? Probably not. First, you might have trouble finding out, and second, unless you are playing behind screens, it's probably not good to let them talk to each other. Confusion may reign. Whatever it means, here is what is suggested.

Pass means a willingness to play in the contract doubled, i.e., (1♣)–2♣–(Dbl)–Pass. You have: ♠3 ♡63 ♢J75 ♣QJ109872.

You may not make it, but it rates to be your best "minus" position. And the bidding isn't over; your LHO might bid.

Redouble means you want partner to pick the contract. You are likely 2–2 in the majors with no suit of your own. If partner is 5–5 it doesn't matter, but if he is 6–5, it's important.

Other bids are basically the same as if RHO had passed. So 3♣, for example, is natural, to play. 3♢ (their suit) also promises clubs, but it suggests a save if the opponents continue to game. Finally, jumps are preemptive.

Players tend to be too conservative, especially at favorable vulnerability. Shape beats points. It's more important to describe the distribution than the strength. Partner will be more likely to do the right thing. Once you have shown your distribution, regardless of strength, you can generally relax. Make the opponents guess what to do next.

RHO bids. After (1♣)–2♣, players use various agreements. If RHO bids 2♡ or 2♠, that usually is either a fragment bid trying for 3NT or saying he has a good hand in support of opener's suit. The third option, a natural bid, is unlikely.

In any case, this usually means you will have little in the way of high-card values. Any action you take will be based on distribution and be competitive or preemptive.

Pass is a significant call in this situation for advancer because your partner should know you would bid if you had an excuse to. She therefore won't bid again without a very good reason.

Double says you have three-card support in the suit RHO bid (if it's a major). This may help your partner compete or direct his opening lead.

Other calls

2♠: possible if RHO bid 2♡. Competing with three-card support.

3♣: a good hand with diamonds, e.g., ♠ 4 ♡ Q 2 ◊ K Q J 9 6 4 2 ♣ 4 3 2.

3◊: Natural, more preemptive, e.g., ♠ 5 3 ♡ 9 8 ◊ K J 10 8 6 5 3 2 ♣ 2.

3♡/3♠: Four-card support. Bid with confidence. K–J–x–x and out is fine.

4♡/4♠: More shape, more trumps. Check the vulnerability.

Note that after (1◊)–2◊, some of the above may not be available.

In a competitive auction, 2NT may not be available. For example, you hold: ♠ Q 3 ♡ 7 5 3 2 ◊ K 6 4 2 ♣ Q J 8, and the auction proceeds as follows: (1♡)–2♡–(partner)–3♡. You desire to compete to four of partner's minor, so bid 4♣. Without clubs, partner should correct to 4◊. If you wanted to play in five of his minor, you would bid 4NT.

Strange sounding auctions: Remember to follow the important treatment ASBAF. What, you don't play this? You better or you will have an unhappy partner. This stands for "All Strange Bids Are Forcing." This is a good principle anytime; if you don't know what partner's bid means, do NOT pass.

Any strange-sounding action denotes a strong two-suiter. A Michaels cue bidder may subsequently (a) cue bid the opponent's suit, (b) bid notrump, (c) bid a suit he cannot possibly have, or (d) double in a competitive auction.

For example, you hold: ♠ K Q 10 5 3 ♡ A J 9 5 3 ◇ A K 6 ♣ —.

Opp	Pard	Opp	You
		1♣	2♣
Pass	2♡	Pass	3◇

The 3◇ bid suggests 5=5=3=0 shape. If partner bids only 3♡, pass is probably best. Another example. This time you hold: ♠ 5 ♡ A Q 10 7 5 ◇ A K Q 7 4 ♣ K 5.

Opp	Pard	Opp	You
		1♠	2♠
Pass	3♣	Pass	3♠

Partner's 3♣ was pass or correct. Over your 3♠ bid, partner may bid 3NT to play, bid 4♣ pass or correct, or bid 4NT to ask for your minor.

Note that as long as the Michaels cue bidder's minor suit is unknown, 4NT is asking for that suit. Otherwise, 4NT would be whatever form of Blackwood.

Further Applications

Besides being used in the direct seat after an opening bid, there are other applications for Michaels. The following presumes that (a) the opponents have opened the bidding; (b) partner has never bid, and (c) it is your first opportunity to bid.

1◇–Pass(partner)–1NT–2◇(you) shows the majors. A typical hand would be: ♠ A 10 9 6 4 ♡ K J 6 4 2 ◇ 3 ♣ 10 4.

Similarly, 1♣–Pass(partner)–1♠–2♣ (you) is a two-suited takeout. Your hand is something like: ♠ 5 ♡ J 10 9 7 4 ◇ K J 10 6 5 ♣ A 4.

Note that the cue bid of your LHO's suit is a distributional take-out. With less shape, i.e., 1=4=5=3 and a good hand, you might double. With a more distributional hand but fewer HCP, i.e., ♠ — ♡ J 10 9 6 5 ◇ K J 10 6 4 2 ♣ 7 3, you would bid the Unusual 2NT which we will discuss later.

Note that bidding RHO's suit is **natural**. You hold this hand: ♠ A K J 10 6 5 ♡ K 7 ◇ 10 7 6 4 ♣ A, and the auction goes 1♣ on your left, partner passes, and 1♠ on your right. Bid 2♠, natural.

Michaels Practice Hands

What do you bid with each of the following hands after LHO opens 1♣, partner bids 2♣ (Michaels) and RHO passes?

(a) ♠ Q 5	♡ 6 4	◇ K 10 6 4 2	♣ K J 6 5
(b) ♠ Q	♡ 8 7	◇ K 10 8 6 4 2	♣ 8 6 5 4
(c) ♠ Q 3	♡ Q 10 7 5	◇ Q 8 6 4 3	♣ 7 5
(d) ♠ Q 3	♡ Q 10 9 6 4	◇ 9 8 6 5	♣ Q 4

(a) 2♡. Partner usually is 5–5 in the majors but may be 5–6. He won't be 6–5. If you were thinking about 3◇, don't tell anyone.

(b) 2♡. Quantity, not quality. Please, I told you: Put the 2◇ card away.

(c) 3♡ (or 4♡ non-vul). Preemptive.

(d) 4♡. More preemptive. Can they make 6♣?

What do you bid with each of the following hands after LHO opens 1♠, partner bids 2♠(Michaels) and RHO passes?

(e) ♠ 10 7 5 3	♡ 2	◇ A 8 6 4 2	♣ J 8 7
(f) ♠ 7 5 3 2	♡ 2	◇ K J 7 5	♣ A 6 4 2
(g) ♠ A 10 9 6	♡ 2	◇ K 4	♣ A K Q 9 6 5

(e) 3♣. Pass or correct, happy to play in clubs or diamonds at the three level.

(f) 4♣. Preemptive, pass or correct.

(g) 3NT. An optimist, even opposite a minimum. Good spade spots.

What do you bid with each of the following hands after LHO opens 1♣, partner bids 2♣ (Michaels) and RHO passes?

(h) ♠ 8 6 ♡ 6 5 ◇ 10 7 5 3 2 ♣ K 9 7 6
(i) ♠ 10 9 7 ♡ 7 ◇ A 8 6 5 4 ♣ J 6 5 2
(j) ♠ 6 5 ♡ 8 4 ◇ K J 8 6 ♣ A Q 5 4 3

(h) 2♡. Weak. And if partner continues with 3♡, showing a strong Michaels, you will pass, as you have no fit and no values.

(i) 2♠. Weak. But if partner presses on with 3♠, you have enough to carry on to 4♠. Yes, your hand is a minimum, but you have three trumps and a cover card.

(j) 2♡. If partner shows a strong hand with 3♡, try 3NT.

What do you bid with each of the following hands after LHO opens 1♡, partner bids 2♡ (Michaels) and RHO passes?

(k) ♠ 5 ♡ 7 5 4 3 ◇ A J 3 2 ♣ K J 5 4
(l) ♠ 5 ♡ 7 5 4 3 ◇ A J 3 2 ♣ K J 5 4

(k) 3♣, pass or correct. If partner raises to 4♣, strong, bid 5♣.

(l) 3♣, pass or correct. But when partner bids 4◇, strong, bid 5◇.

Agreements Over Their Michaels

You need to have agreements when the opponents bid Michaels. We have discussed some. Some final thoughts.

If partner opens 1♣ and your RHO bids 2♣:

2♢ : 5 - 6 diamonds, 8 – 10 HCP

3♢ : 6 – 7 diamonds, 9 – 11 HCP

If partner opens 1♢ and RHO bids 2♢

3♣ : 6 – 7 clubs, 9 – 11 HCP

None of these bids are forcing. You merely need to show your hand before the bidding gets out of control.

Other bids, like raising partner we have discussed.

Example: After 1♣ - RHO bids 2♣, bid 3♢ with:

♠ K 6 ♡ 8 7 ♢ K Q J 6 4 2 ♣ 8 6 4

LEAPING MICHAELS

Our discussion of Michaels would not be complete without looking at the following two further extensions.

Leaping Michaels is used to describe two-suited hands when the opponents have opened with a preemptive bid. It is most commonly used over weak two-bids, but can be also used over some opening three-bids.

First, a digression: A common misconception is that after the opponents open a weak two-bid in a major, that Michaels applies at the three level, such as (2♡)–3♡. This defensive bid is best used as an asking bid, with a hand such as this:
♠ K 6 ♡ 6 5 ◇ A K ♣ A K Q 10 9 7 6. This hand has a source of running tricks, and if partner has a heart stopper, 3NT is an obvious target.

The same 2=2=2=7 pattern with 19 HCP but with a club suit looking like ♣ A J 9 6 4 3 2 would start with double first, as there are not nine running tricks opposite a single heart stopper.

Leaping Michaels applies after a 2♡/2♠ opening by your RHO as follows:

A jump to 4♣ shows clubs and the unbid major.
A jump to 4◇ shows diamonds and the unbid major.

Obviously, one needs extra values because these are highly slam-invitational at the four level. A typical hand to bid 4♣ after 2♡ might be one such as this:
♠ A K 10 6 5 ♡ 6 ◇ 3 ♣ K Q 10 9 6 5.

The same meaning would apply in the pass-out seat, i.e., 2♡–Pass–Pass–4♣.

What about after the opponents open 2◇ as a weak 2-bid?

A "leap" to 4♣ = clubs and hearts.
A "leap" to 4◇ = clubs and spades.

A variation played by some pairs is that 4♣ = clubs and a major; 4◇ asks.

Over opening three-bids:

After the opponents open 3♣:
4♣ = Both majors.
4♢ = Diamonds and one major.
4♡ = Pass or correct.

After the opponents open 3♢:
4♣ = Clubs and one major.
4♢ = Both majors.

Extended Leaping Michaels

In the May 2020 issue of *The Bridge World* magazine, the panel was presented with this problem. What do you bid after the auction 1♢–Pass–Pass with:
♠ A K J 10 x ♡ A ♢ K ♣ K J 10 x x x?

The panel was equally divided between double and 2♣, with everyone admitting their bids had serious flaws. So in the April 2021 issue, Michael Becker suggested *Extended Leaping Michaels*:

After one of a minor–Pass–Pass:
4♣ = hearts and the unbid minor.
4♢ = spades and the unbid minor.

After one of a major–Pass–Pass:
4♣ = clubs and the unbid major.
4♢ = diamonds and the unbid major.

He suggested that these methods could also be applied in direct or reopening position after a natural two of a minor opening or by fourth hand after the opponents offer a weak raise of a natural one of a minor to two.

In advancing, a one-step bid asks partner to bid his major. 4NT is a key-card ask for the major. Thanks, Michael Becker.

Can you imagine what Mike Michaels would think if he were alive today and could see how far his convention has come?

THE MODERN GAME

With both vulnerable, South holds: ♠A J 10 9 7 ♡5 4 ◊A 10 8 6 5 ♣2.

West	North	East	South
		1♡	1♠
2♠	Pass	4♡	?

East opened, and South overcalled. West showed a good hand for hearts, and East bid game. As South, would you bid or pass? In the example, South overcalled the first time because he had learned to use Michaels with either weak hands or very strong hands. He felt that this hand, however, fell in the middle range. He passed. E/W +620. Is this the right approach?

No. Shape rules. It's much more important to show shape than worry about your high-card strength. I have one student who was adamant about not bidding Michaels with this hand. That's just wrong. It's fine if the bidding comes back to you in two hearts but compare it to this auction:

West	North	East	South
		1♡	2♡
2♠	4NT	Pass	5◊

Here, South bids Michaels and West shows some constructive heart raise. But North knows to ask for South's minor, and from that point, it's E/W's problem. 5◊ doubled is a good save, while 5♡ is down one with proper defense:

West	North	East
	♠4	
	♡2	
	◊Q J 4 3 2	
	♣J 9 7 6 5 4	
♠K 8 6 2		♠Q 5 3
♡A J 9 8		♡K Q 10 7 6 3
◊9 7		◊K
♣A Q 10		♣K 8 3
	♠A J 10 9 7	
	♡5 4	
	◊A 10 8 6 5	
	♣2	

HAND EVALUATION

As South, you hold: ♠Q 7 5 3 ♡10 ◇9 8 2 ♣A 8 5 3 2.

West	North	East	South
1◇	2◇	Pass	?

West opened 1◇ and your partner bid 2◇, both majors. OK, up to you. What's it going to be, Alfie?

North could have any strength hand. The idea of limiting two-suited overcalls to weak hands (8–10 HCP) or strong hands (16+ HCP), while still adhered to in some circles, has pretty much been abandoned. Shape over strength.

It's much more important to disrupt the opponents' bidding process when you have a distributional hand of any strength. The chances of finding a fit with your partner are often good. A cheap save or just the ability to disrupt their auction is too valuable. We will worry about the points later.

OK, I've stalled long enough; you should have decided what to bid. How many spades? I hope not just two. This is a good hand. You have four trumps and an ace. No, you don't have to bid game, but certainly this is worth a 3♠ bid.

After all, think about what hand you might bid 2♠ on. A hand that looks like ♠Q x x ♡x x x ◇Q x x ♣Q J x x. That hand actually has more points than the other one.

Say North's hand was ♠A K 9 4 2 ♡A Q J 8 7 ◇5 4 ♣J. Hearing your jump to 3♠, North bids 4♠. He would have passed 2♠.

MUST I BID?

You hold: ♠Q 10 ♡3 2 ♢J 10 9 6 ♣A J 7 6 4.

Your LHO opens 1♣, and partner bids 2♣ for the majors. Of course, you are pulling for RHO to bid, but of course, he passes. Just great. Can you pass? Could 2♣ be the best spot?

No, you would need at least six or more clubs and a nice suit. You might be trading your known 5–2 major fit (or even 6–2) for a 5–1 club fit. Try to keep from acting displeased and bid in tempo.

Which major did you choose? Your robust doubleton spades or your tiny doubleton hearts? (You didn't try to get out in 2NT, did you? That's an artificial asking bid, not a home.)

I hope you picked the tiny hearts. You are searching for quantity, not quality. You want to be in the suit with the most number of trumps. Partner likely has equal length, but if one suit is longer, it's hearts.

If overcaller has six spades and five hearts, he often is better overcalling in spades first. But with five spades and six hearts, overcalling in hearts will lose the spade suit.

Bid a confident 2♡. Hey, I didn't hear anybody double yet.

North's hand is: ♠K J 9 6 3 ♡A Q 8 6 5 4 ♢8 ♣5.

THE SIGNIFICANCE OF COVER CARDS

You are South. You hold: ♠6 2 ♡Q 8 3 2 ◊K 8 4 3 ♣A K 4.

West opens the bidding 1♣, and your partner bids 2♣, Michaels, showing both majors. You are pleased to have a heart fit. What do you think your hand is worth? 2♡? 3♡? Other?

It's hard to say. What's good about your hand and what's bad? West rates to have the ◊A, so your king may be worthless. That's the bad news. Everything else is rosy!

Four trumps, a ruffing value in spades and the ♣A K, which are two cover cards to take care of two of partner's minor-suit cards. He likely only has three minor-suit cards at the most. If partner has just five hearts to the king and five spades to the king, game is certainly possible.

Bid a confident 4♡ and expect to be making your contract:

	North	
	♠A Q 8 4 3 ♡K J 9 7 4 ◊5 ♣8 3	
West ♠K 9 ♡A 6 ◊A Q 7 ♣J 10 9 6 5 2		**East** ♠J 10 7 5 ♡10 5 ◊J 10 9 6 2 ♣Q 7
	♠6 2 ♡Q 8 3 2 ◊K 8 4 3 ♣A K 4	

North has only 10 HCP, but with distribution, you might make an overtrick.

Cover cards (sure winners) are great to cover side suits. Kings and queens in the side suits may turn out to be worthless.

GOING NOWHERE

With none vulnerable, North picks up: ♠9 8 ♡Q 8 3 ♢A 5 3 ♣A 10 6 4 2.

East	South	West	North
1♡	2♡	Pass	?

South is showing spades and a minor. North is certainly not interested in going very far. How should he continue?

This depends on partnership agreements. We discussed several options. Some play that 2NT asks partner to bid his minor. As we pointed out, this bid is much better used as a game try in partner's major.

So how does North find partner's minor? With no game interest, North simply bids 3♣. Partner will pass with clubs or bid 3♢ with diamonds. This is called "pass or correct." The full deal:

	North	
	♠9 8 ♡Q 8 3 ♢A 5 3 ♣A 10 6 4 2	
♠6 3 2 ♡10 5 4 2 ♢10 6 2 ♣Q J 8		♠A Q 5 ♡A K J 9 7 ♢J 9 ♣K 5 3
	♠K J 10 7 4 ♡6 ♢K Q 8 7 4 ♣9 7	

After North bids 3♣, South corrects to 3♢ ending the auction.

GIVE IT A TRY

With only your side vulnerable, you hold this hand as South:

♠A 10 6 3 2 ♡Q 6 2 ◇A 8 ♣7 6 5.

West	North	East	South
1♡	2♡	Pass	?

How much is the South hand worth? The hand has lots of trumps, but should South blast into game? South is red against white: Maybe 3♠ is high enough?

How about just making a game try with 2NT? Get some more information; involve partner (so you can blame him if things go wrong!). The auction could continue as such:

West	North	East	South	
1♡	2♡	Pass	2NT*	(*game try)
Pass	3◇	Pass	4♠	
All Pass				

If partner's second suit is diamonds, game is likely on, losing three tricks in hearts and clubs:

	♠K Q 9 5 4 ♡7 5 ◇K J 10 9 4 ♣3	
♠J ♡A K J 10 4 ◇Q 6 2 ♣A Q 10 8		♠8 7 ♡9 8 3 ◇7 5 3 ♣K J 9 4 2
	♠A 10 6 3 2 ♡Q 6 2 ◇A 8 ♣7 6 5	

PASS-OUT SEAT

North holds: ♠2 ♡QJ85 ◇K952 ♣9643.

West	North	East	South
1♡	Pass	Pass	2♡
Pass	?		

What is South doing? It used to be that this auction showed a really big take-out hand, usually with a void. Because partner was afraid North would pass the double for penalty, the cue bid was used instead. It showed a hand South wanted to be sure to declare, not defend.

But this came up so infrequently that most pairs now play this as Michaels, the same as in the direct seat.

With that in mind, what should North bid?

North should bid 3♣, to play in whichever minor South has.

South will likely pass with clubs or correct to diamonds unless he has a really strong hand.

South's hand: ♠K9753 ♡A9 ◇3 ♣KQJ107.

WHAT'S HE UP TO?

North holds: ♠4 ♡Q 10 5 ◇Q 8 7 6 4 ♣10 6 4 2.

West	North	East	South
1♣	Pass	1NT	2♣
Pass	?		

What should North do? Well, of course that depends if North knows what South is showing with the 2♣ bid. What do you think? Clubs?

Of course, I had the South hand playing with a student. She raised to 3♣, later telling me I told her to always try to raise with trump support. I guess I'm lucky she didn't jump to 4♣, preemptive.

As a general rule, one never wants to play in a suit bid on your left. 2♣, of course, is a Michaels Cue Bid.

	North	
	♠4 ♡Q 10 5 ◇Q 8 7 6 4 ♣10 6 4 2	
West ♠A 7 3 2 ♡6 2 ◇A J 5 ♣A 9 8 7		**East** ♠J 9 8 ♡K 7 4 ◇K 10 3 2 ♣J 5 3
	♠K Q 10 6 5 ♡A J 9 8 3 ◇9 ♣K Q	

DELAYED MICHAELS

North holds: ♠10 2 ♡K 9 4 2 ◇A 10 9 2 ♣Q J 10.

West	North	East	South
			Pass
1♣	Pass	1◇	2♣
Dbl	?		

South, a passed hand, is bidding 2♣. Is that clubs or some strange cue bid from Mars? What should North do?

First, let's dismiss the idea that South has clubs. A good rule to remember is you does not want to play in the suit on your left, the suit that is "over" you or "behind" you. If you have A–Q–10–8–6, you can, if you have to, handle K–J–9–7 on your right, but not on your left.

Bidding the suit on your right can be natural, as in an auction such as this: 1♣–Pass–1♡–2♡. That's natural; you have hearts. An example hand:

♠3 ◇A 4 ♡A K J 10 7 5 ♣K Q 5 4.

So partner's 2♣ call here is a delayed Michaels Cue Bid for the majors. Since South is a passed hand, game is unlikely, but North can compete vigorously in hearts, up to 3♡ if necessary.

South's hand: ♠A J 7 6 3 ♡Q J 7 6 3 ◇7 3 ♣3.

WHO IS SAVING? WHO IS MAKING?

With both sides vulnerable, West holds: ♠K Q 10 7 3 ♡A Q J 8 3 ◊8 2 ♣Q.

West	North	East	South
			1♣
2♣	5♣	5♠	6♣
?			

South opened and everyone joined in the bidding fest. By the time the bidding got back to West, the opponents were in 6♣.

Just great! Now what? Bid, pass or double? If you choose to bid, what suit will you bid? More spades?

Who is bidding to make and who is saving? What do you think? Decide before going on.

West	North	East
	♠9	
	♡10 7 6 4 2	
	◊4	
	♣A J 9 8 5 3	
♠K Q 10 7 3		♠J 6 5 4
♡A Q J 8 3		♡K 9 5
◊8 2		◊K J 10 9 6 5
♣Q		♣—
	♠A 8 2	
	♡—	
	◊A Q 7 3	
	♣K 10 7 6 4 2	

What did you pick? Double? That will get -1740, a rather uncommon score. Did East pull your double to 6♠, which South can double for -500 ... unless South bids 7♣.

DEFEND OR SAVE?

With E/W vul, North holds: ♠10 4 2 ♡10 9 8 3 ♢A 6 4 ♣K 9 4.

West	North	East	South
		1♡	2♡
3♡	3♠	4♡	Pass
Pass	?		

Are you done? You have four trumps. Do you want to defend or declare, taking a save? What's your decision?

	North	
	♠10 4 2 ♡10 9 8 3 ♢A 6 4 ♣K 9 4	
♠K 8 ♡Q J 5 ♢Q J 9 3 2 ♣10 5 3		♠A 7 3 ♡A K 6 4 2 ♢K 10 7 ♣J 7
	♠Q J 9 6 5 ♡7 ♢8 5 ♣A Q 8 6 2	

With so many hearts being bid, North should be quite certain South has one at the most. He also knows he has a filler honor for whichever is partner's minor.

But the biggest factor for saving is the favorable vulnerability, white vs red.

If E/W are making 4♡, down three in 4♠ will be a good sacrifice. And if E/W carry on to 5♡, N/S will have a plus score.

FITS AND COVERS

With none vulnerable, South holds: ♠Q 9 7 ♡K 8 7 6 ◇K Q J 3 ♣K 4.

West	North	East	South
1♣	2♣	Pass	?

South knew he had a double fit in the majors and lots of points, so he bid 4♡. The full deal:

	North	
	♠A J 6 5 3 ♡A Q 10 3 2 ◇10 ♣8 5	
West ♠J 9 ♡5 4 ◇A 8 5 ♣A Q J 10 9 7		**East** ♠K 4 2 ♡10 8 ◇9 7 6 4 2 ♣6 3 2
	♠Q 9 7 ♡K 8 7 6 ◇K Q J 3 ♣K 4	

South lost three tricks in the minors, and when the spade finesse lost, he was down one. "Unlucky, partner," said North. "None of your high cards took a trick."

Yes, it was unlucky that the finesse lost. But compare this to the previous hand. It also had a double fit, but that hand, with only 8 HCP, had an ace, a cover card that took a trick and it obtained a good result.

This hand has 14 HCP, a lot more, and there was a pretty good dummy. But all these kings and queens opposite shortness don't take many tricks. One or two aces – good cover cards, as they are sure winners — would have been worth a lot more.

UNDERSTANDING PASS

With both sides vul., North holds: ♠A 9 8 7 2 ♡K Q J 8 3 ♢8 ♣7 2.

West	North	East	South
1♢	2♢	Dbl	Pass
Pass	?		

It's your call. Mike Lawrence once said that "there are bidding situations that are as tense and full of tragedy as a Shakespearean play." This is certainly one of them. Do you know what your partner's pass means without peeking?

Are you supposed to pick a major, or does partner want to play in 2♢ doubled? Do you think this is an important question?

You better believe it. Here is a solid agreement you need to have: Pass is to play; redouble says, "You pick,"; the other minor is to play. Period, curtain falls.

West	North	East
	♠A 9 8 7 2	
	♡K Q J 8 3	
	♢8	
	♣7 2	
♠J 10 4		♠K Q 6 3
♡A 4		♡10 9 7 6 5
♢Q 9 5 3		♢A
♣A Q 8 3		♣10 9 5
	♠5	
	♡2	
	♢K J 10 7 6 4 2	
	♣K J 6 4	

This 'Shakespearean' play received bad reviews in the papers, but it probably could have been worse.

GOTTA BE RIGHT

With both sides vul., South holds: ♠ 7 6 2 ♡ A 9 7 6 2 ◊ K 8 5 4 ♣ 9.

West	North	East	South
1♠	2♠	3♠	4♡
4♠	Pass	Pass	?

Should South bid again? Bidding four then five is usually wrong. It typically means you should have bid five the first time. But East is vulnerable, and with fear of -800, he passed.

What do you think?

South should anticipate one spade loser and probable two minor-suit losers. When he bid 4♡, he was bidding to make, not to save.

If you think E/W are making four spades for +620, 5♡ doubled has to be a good save.

	North	
	♠ 9	
	♡ K J 10 5 4	
	◊ 6 2	
	♣ K Q 10 7 4	
♠ K J 10 5 3		♠ A Q 8 4
♡ Q		♡ 8 3
◊ A 9		◊ Q J 10 7 3
♣ A J 8 6 2		♣ 5 3
	♠ 7 6 2	
	♡ A 9 7 6 2	
	◊ K 8 5 4	
	♣ 9	

CHECK THE VULNERABILITY

East holds: ♠5 4 2 ♡K 10 7 4 ◊Q 9 ♣J 8 4 2.

North	East	South	West
	Pass	1♠	2♠
4♡*	?		

*Splinter in support of spades

As East are you bidding or passing? If you pass, South will bid 4♠ (or more). How many tricks do you think you will lose in 5♡?

Partner has a singleton spade on the bidding, so you'll lose one spade, probably no hearts, and two or three tricks in the minors. If South has clubs, you have a nine-card fit. If South has diamonds, you expect to lose only one diamond. So what to do?

If down one, great but how about down two? Is that OK? Now it's time, if you haven't already, to check the vulnerability.

At equal, down two, -300 against -420, or -500 against -620 would be acceptable. But if red against while, down two would be terrible:

	North	
	♠J 10 8 6 ♡6 ◊A 6 5 ♣K Q 10 7 3	
♠3 ♡A Q 8 3 2 ◊K J 8 4 2 ♣9 6		♠5 4 2 ♡K 10 7 4 ◊Q 9 ♣J 8 4 2
	♠A K Q 9 7 ♡J 9 5 ◊10 7 3 ♣A 5	

FANCY FOOTWORK

<table>
<tr><td></td><td>♠A K 10 8 6 3
♡K Q 10 9 6
◇8
♣7</td><td></td></tr>
<tr><td>♠J 5
♡J 8 7
◇A K Q 10
♣Q J 10 8</td><td></td><td>♠9 4
♡5 4
◇J 6 3 2
♣K 5 4 3 2</td></tr>
<tr><td></td><td>♠Q 7 2
♡A 3 2
◇9 7 5 4
♣A 9 6</td><td></td></tr>
</table>

West	North	East	South
1◇	2◇	Pass	2NT
Pass	3NT	Pass	4♣
Pass	4NT	Pass	5♠
Pass	6♠	All Pass	

West opened 1◇ and North bid 2◇, the Michaels Cue Bid, showing at least 5–5 in the majors, of indeterminate strength. Using the scheme as described by Mike Lawrence in the chapter on Responding to Michaels, South bid 2NT asking for more description.

North bid 3NT to show a maximum with longer spades. When South bid 4♣, a cue bid, North checked for key cards and bid 6♠.

"I didn't expect to be the dummy," said North, putting down his hand.

"We have been waiting a long time for Mike's treatment to come up, partner," said South. "Did you think I wouldn't remember the responses?" asked North.

TAKING YOUR LUMPS

With N/S vul South holds: ♠5 4 ♡2 ♢K 10 9 6 5 3 ♣Q 9 6 5.

West	North	East	South
1♢	2♢	Pass	?

What should South be thinking about bidding? Certainly, 2♢ was not what he was hoping to hear. How big is the penalty going to be if the final contract is doubled, whatever that turns out to be? Should he bid 2♠ and take one for the team or pass 2♢?

2♢ is probably not making, and 2♠ may likely be a better contract, BUT – can he stop in 2♠? There is a good chance North will raise. And it might be difficult for the opponents to double 2♢. I think pass is best. The whole deal:

West	North	East
	♠K J 10 9 8	
	♡A K Q 8 3	
	♢J	
	♣K 8	
♠A 6 3 2		♠Q 7
♡6 4		♡J 10 9 7 5
♢A Q 8 7 2		♢4
♣A 10		♣J 7 4 3 2
	♠5 4	
	♡2	
	♢K 10 9 6 5 3	
	♣Q 9 6 5	

If South bids 2♠, you can't blame North for bidding 3♠ or 4♠. And if you pass, West may be reluctant to double, fearing East will bid. Who knows? (Only the Shadow?)

As Mike Lawrence always says, better to take it in small lumps than big ones.

ASKING FOR WHAT?

North holds: ♠10 7 5 2 ♡9 2 ◊Q 9 8 2 ♣K 8 3.

East	South	West	North
2◊	3◊	Pass	?

Your LHO has opened a weak two-bid in diamonds, and partner bid 3◊. What's going on? What are you going to do?

Is partner asking for a stopper? North remembered that after two of a major, three of a major asks partner to bid 3NT with a stopper. Some players get confused, thinking an auction like 2♡–3♡ is a Michaels Cue Bid, which it is not. That *does* ask for a stopper. Is this the same?

No. Over a minor preempt, a cue bid is for the majors, saying you have a good enough hand to compete at the level you are bidding. In that light, what should North bid? It's close: 3♠ or 4♠. Remember, having four trumps in these auctions is big. The whole deal:

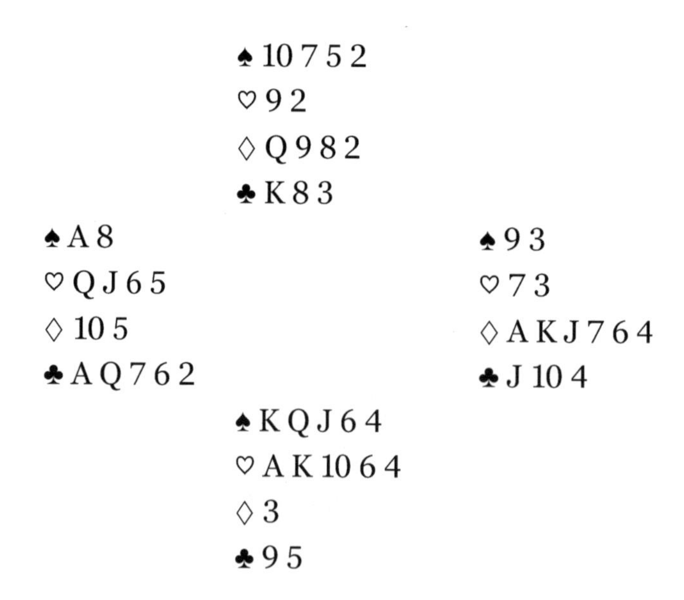
♠10 7 5 2
♡9 2
◊Q 9 8 2
♣K 8 3

West	East
♠A 8	♠9 3
♡Q J 6 5	♡7 3
◊10 5	◊A K J 7 6 4
♣A Q 7 6 2	♣J 10 4

♠K Q J 6 4
♡A K 10 6 4
◊3
♣9 5

Notice that even with North's meager assets, 4♠ is not a terrible contract.

HIGHER

	♠K 10 7 3 ♡A ◊8 3 ♣10 8 7 6 4 2	
♠Q 9 5 ♡J 9 8 5 3 ◊K 5 4 ♣K 5		♠4 ♡4 ◊A Q J 10 9 7 2 ♣Q J 9 3
	♠A J 8 6 2 ♡K Q 10 7 6 2 ◊6 ♣A	

West	*North*	*East*	*South*
		3◊	4◊
Pass	4♠	All Pass	

On the previous deal, we saw South bidding 3◊ over East's 2◊. Here is just further extension of high-level Michaels, just needing more distribution and more support points because you are forcing partner to game.

Partner bids 4♠. Are you done?

Yes. You can see all four hands and it's a pretty good slam. North has to guess the trump suit. But North would have also bid 4♠ holding:
♠Q 6 4 ♡9 3 ◊K 8 7 2 ♣J 9 8 4, in which case game would be plenty high.

It's tough over preempts.

Remember what the great Al Roth said: "The purpose of bidding is to get to the best possible contract. After preempts, it's to get to the best contract possible." There is a big difference.

DRAGGING PARTNER TO THE TROUGH

West	North	East	South
		2♢	3♢*
Pass	4♣^	Pass	4♢**
Pass	4♠^^	All Pass	

* Michaels (majors)

^ Not interested in the majors

** More Michaels

^^ All right, already

Sometimes it's hard to get your partner to do what you want. East opened 2♢, and South bid 3♢ for the majors. North bid his own seven-card suit. South bid 4♢, more Michaels, saying PLEASE bid a major. North took a reluctant preference to 4♠.

The whole deal:

West	North	East
	♠ 10 9	
	♡ 9	
	♢ A 6 3	
	♣ K Q 9 7 6 3	
♠ 8 5		♠ J 4 3
♡ A K 6 5 4 2		♡ 3
♢ K 10 4		♢ J 9 8 7 5 2
♣ 5 2		♣ A 10 8
	♠ A K Q 7 6 2	
	♡ Q J 10 8 7	
	♢ Q	
	♣ J	

LEAPIN' LIZARDS

South holds: ♠A Q J 10 5 ♡3 ♢8 ♣A K J 9 8 3.

West	North	East	South
		2♡	?

South, who has a really nice hand, is thinking game or slam, but in which suit? How should he begin to describe this hand? What are some possible bids?

How about 2♠? Is that forcing? No, and the hand is too strong. What about 3♡? Is that Michaels? Or does it ask partner to bid 3NT with a heart stopper? It's the latter. And if West raises to 4♡, then what?

And the answer is?

This is a perfect hand for Leaping Michaels. 4♣, shows a very good hand with five or more clubs and at least five of the other major, a hand needing very little to make game.

North bids 4♠. Are you done?

Yes, you have described your hand perfectly. If partner had slam interest, he might have made a heart cue bid. Your 4♣ was highly invitational but not forcing. Partner could have passed if he was broke and had no spade fit.

North's hand: ♠9 8 2 ♡Q 9 6 ♢Q 9 5 2 ♣10 4 2.

GREAT BALLS OF FIRE

With none vulnerable, North holds: ♠Q 9 7 6 ♡Q 9 7 2 ♢K 3 2 ♣Q 6

West	North	East	South
		2♢	4♢
Pass	?		

What should North bid? The auction certainly sounded like a simple Michaels auction, South asking for North to bid a major. North bid 4♡. Everyone passed. Do you agree before peeking?

If South wanted to bid Michaels, what call would he have made? Yes, 3♢. So what's 4♢? Better review your notes. Leaping Michaels, a major-minor combo. 4♣ = clubs and hearts, 4♢ = clubs and spades. Whoops.

South wasn't sure what to do over North's 4♡ bid. Sounded like a lot of hearts and he had three hearts so he passed.

West might have bid 5♢ over 4♢, but he thought maybe there was an accident coming. He was right. Leapin' lizards.

	North	
	♠Q 9 7 6 ♡Q 9 7 2 ♢K 3 2 ♣Q 6	
♠K 2 ♡K J 10 8 6 ♢8 6 5 4 ♣10 7		♠8 4 ♡5 ♢A Q J 10 9 7 ♣5 4 3 2
	♠A J 10 5 3 ♡A 4 3 ♢— ♣A K J 9 8	

CHAPTER 4
The Unusual Notrump

THE UNUSUAL NOTRUMP

One of the first conventions new players learn is the Unusual Notrump. Most commonly, this is a jump to 2NT over an opponent's one-level opening, showing a two-suited hand, specifically, the two lowest unbid suits.

This treatment was originally devised by Alvin Roth with Tobias Stone in 1948 to show the minor suits after an opponent had opened one of a major. In his classic book, The Roth–Stone System, Roth was the first to advocate weak jump overcalls and responses when standard practice was for those bids to show strong hands.

He recommended protective bidding tactics to not allow the opponents to play low-level contracts. One included the use of 2NT as an overcall to show minor-suit holdings with 5–5 or 5–4 shape, allowing advancer to choose. If necessary, advancer had to bid a three-card suit, but this served as a warning against bidding the unbid major.

The drawbacks of the convention are twofold, the same as with Michaels. The opponents may double and collect more by defending than declaring. The other is the additional information may provide a roadmap for a declarer in the play of the hand.

As far as strength, vulnerability, etc, everything we have discussed in regard to Michaels applies here as well. These calls are not Alertable.

Over 1♡/1♠:	2NT = minors
Over 1♣:	2NT = diamonds and hearts
Over 1◇:	2NT = clubs and hearts

Note that the Unusual Notrump is almost always a *jump* bid. This is often one of the most misunderstood bids in bridge. When the opponents open a weak two-bid, a 2NT overcall is not a jump bid. It is a natural call, a hand that would have opened 1NT if possible, showing 15 HCP up to 18 HCP, balanced, with the weak two-bidder's suit well stopped.

What do you need to bid the Unusual Notrump?

It starts with shape, at least 5–5 and competitive values. What does that mean? You need some values, but not too many. Don't get too concerned about an exact number of high-card points. Location of honor cards and suit texture are far more important.

For example, consider these hands:

(a) ♠3 ♡6 4 ◇K Q J 5 4 ♣J 10 9 8 7
(b) ♠K ♡Q 5 ◇K Q 7 5 3 ♣9 7 6 5 4

Hand (a) has 7 HCP, Hand (b) has 10 HCP. But Hand (a) is a fine hand to overcall 2NT at equal or favorable vulnerability. Hand (b) is totally unsuitable. It has too many points in the short suits. The ♠K and the ♡Q will be of little value to partner when he is doubled in 3♣, but they likely will stop the opponents from making a slam. Also, the disparity in suit quality screams pass.

Another example of "points, schmoints":

(c) ♠2 ♡6 ◇Q J 10 8 7 ♣J 10 9 8 5 4
(d) ♠K ♡A J ◇Q 7 5 3 2 ♣J 8 6 4 2

Hand (c) with four HCP is good for the Unusual Notrump, but Hand (d) with eleven HCP is not.

What about the vulnerability? It's not only a practical difference but a psychological one as well. When you are vul against non-vul opponents, they will be much more interested in trying to double for penalty.

Suit quality (good spot cards) is what often keeps you from getting doubled. There is a big difference between defending with a trump holding of K–5–4–3–2 and K–J–9–7–6.

Examples of vul vs non-vul hands worth bidding 2NT over one of a major:

♠6 3 ♡3 ◇A K 7 6 5 ♣Q 10 9 7 5
♠3 ♡7 6 ◇K J 10 5 4 ♣K Q J 10 5
♠4 ♡A 5 ◇K Q 10 4 3 ♣Q J 10 6 2

There can be confusion after a 1♣ opening by the opponents, namely, when the opponents are playing an artificial club or short club. If 1♣ is natural, then 2NT shows diamonds and hearts. If 1♣ or 1♢ "could just be short," (as few as two clubs), also treat the opening as natural.

If it's a conventional call, where 1♣ doesn't say anything about club length, such as in the Precision system, then 2NT shows the minors. Likewise, if their 1♢ opening could show one or zero diamonds, as in some versions of Precision, then 2NT shows the minors.

Over a strong, artificial 2♣, 2NT is Unusual for the minors. But when a Precision pair opens 2♣, showing six-plus clubs and 11–15 HCP, then 2NT may still be played as Unusual (diamonds and hearts), even though it's not a jump. For example:
♠Q 7 6 ♡A 10 9 5 3 ♢A J 10 6 5 ♣— .

Any 2NT bid over any weak or intermediate two-level opening is natural, as discussed, showing a strong notrump.

More Unusual 2NT Bids

Any 2NT by a passed hand is Unusual, e.g., Pass–(1♠)–Pass–(Pass); 2NT.

2NT is Unusual when partner's take-out double has been redoubled, as in this auction: (1♣)–Dbl–(Redbl)–2NT. This shows hearts and diamonds, probably longer diamonds.

A competitive 2NT after denying strength is Unusual:

West	North	East	South
1♡	1♠	2♡	2♠
Pass	Pass	2NT	

In this auction, a competitive double by East instead of 2NT would show strength, but with: ♠ — ♡Q 5 4 ♢Q 8 6 4 2 ♣Q 10 7 5 3, an Unusual 2NT describes this hand well.

The Unusual Notrump is possible even when both opponents have bid. After an auction such as (1♡)–Pass–(1♠), 2NT would still show the minors, e.g., a 1=2=5=5 hand which, depending on the vulnerability, lacks strength. With a better hand, you might make a take-out double. 2NT is more preemptive.

For example, after (1♣)–Pass–(1NT), 2NT would show the two lowest unbid suits, diamonds and hearts. After (1♡)–Pass–2◇, 2NT is Unusual, but it shows extra length and/or strength, as the 2NT bidder is entering a 2/1 auction.

By a passed hand, 1NT can be unusual. After Pass–(1♡)–Pass–(1♠), 1NT shows at least 5–5 in the minors. 2NT sends the same message, but 1NT may be enough.

Finally, after an auction such as Pass–(Pass)–Pass–(1◇), 1NT is Unusual, showing hearts and clubs, while 2◇ would be Michaels, showing both majors.

3NT and 4NT Overcalls

3NT overcalls are almost always natural, to play, and have a wide range. They can be big, balanced hands, or, perhaps, hands with fewer high cards but with a source of tricks, usually in a long running minor suit.

4NT overcalls are for take-out, usually the minors, but can show any two-suited hand. Over low-level bids, 4NT overcalls are similar to 2NT only with more shape, and therefore are more preemptive. Over opening four-bids, 4NT overcalls are usually very strong hands.

RESPONDING TO THE UNUSUAL NOTRUMP

As with other two-suited bids, if responder has a fit, she should try to bid to the appropriate level as fast as possible. With a weak hand and at least four-card support, consider making a preemptive jump raise. With no fit and RHO passing, bid the longer of the two suits. If equal, bid the lower.

With a good hand, partner can cue bid the opponent's suit. This generally shows support for at least one of partner's suits, and interest in game or slam. A cue bid is forcing for one round and asks the 2NT bidder to bid his cheapest suit at the cheapest level with a weak hand, or make a different call with extra values.

All raises are natural and non-forcing. All other bids show a good hand, but with the exception of a cue bid are non-forcing.

The bid of the fourth suit, if there is one, is natural and non-forcing. Advancer is showing a very good suit of her own with no support for either of the 2NT bidder's suits.

One of the situations that the Unusual Notrump fails to cover (as does Michaels) is when overcaller has spades and a minor, and the opening bid is one of a minor. Michaels shows the majors, 2NT shows hearts and the other minor. One has to bid spades and hope to bid the other suit later.

Bailey Cue Bids (invented some time ago by Evan Bailey and Ed Barlow) may be used with the Unusual Notrump, a treatment called BUNT. This treatment has some degree of popularity, as the approach is useful in solving the 'spades and another' problem. Without going into detail, BUNT bids differ mainly in the meaning of cue bids of one of a minor. For example, (1♣)–2♣, shows spades and either hearts or diamonds, and (1♢)–2♢ shows spades and either hearts or clubs. For continuations, there is a good article online by Michael Angelo Ravera discussing BUNT in detail.

Like any convention, abuse and overuse of the Unusual Notrump is a good way to demoralize your partner. Too often she has the other two suits. As mentioned, the Unusual 2NT can be more help to the opponents. The best time to use this treatment is when you feel you "must" do something. The idea is not just getting into the bidding, but to get in more accurately.

THE UNUSUAL NOTRUMP BY THE OFFENSE

Sometimes the offense can put the Unusual Notrump to its advantage:

West	North	East	South
			Pass
3♡	Dbl	Pass	4NT

South is showing a good two-suited hand in the minors, just short of an opening bid. North may be able to jump to 6♣ or 6♢.

West	North	East	South
			1♣
4♠	4NT		

When the auction has been crowded, 4NT is usually take-out. 4NT shows a hand like: ♠ — ♡ K Q 7 5 3 ♢ A J 9 8 5 ♣ 7 5 3, indicating a desire to play at the five level, a free choice left to partner.

West	North	East	South
			1♣
1♡	Pass	4♡	4NT

South is likely to have five diamonds and six clubs. 4NT is his only way to indicate this distribution.

West	North	East	South
			1♢
1♠	Pass	4♠	4NT

South's second suit must be hearts. With a minor two-suiter, he would bid 5♣ to offer an easy choice at the five level.

West	North	East	South
			1♡
1♠	Pass	2♠	Pass
Pass	2NT		

North cannot wish to play in 2NT when he could not bid over 1♠. He has a weak minor two-suiter.

THE UNUSUAL NOTRUMP OVER WEAK TWO-BIDS

By now, most players have learned that the auction (2♡/2♠)–2NT is NOT the Unusual Notrump, but rather a hand that would have opened 1NT given the opportunity. This shows a balanced hand, a good 15 to 18 HCP, with the opponent's suit well stopped. This is a more important hand to be able to show than one that's two-suited in the minors.

We also discussed that after 2♡/2♠, an immediate cue bid is NOT Michaels, but rather a good hand with a long, strong minor, asking partner to bid 3NT with a stopper. For example, after RHO opens 2♡, one should bid 3♡ holding:
♠A J ♡7 6 ◇Q 10 ♣A K Q J 7 6 5, which has a big source of tricks, but double with:
♠A J ♡10 6 ◇K Q ♣A J 9 7 6 5 4. This hand has the same shape and high cards but not a source of tricks that can take nine with a heart stopper in partner's hand.

Leaping Michaels is available at the four level with good major/minor hands.

Can we show minors after a weak two-bid? If the hand is strong enough, 4NT can be played as the Unusual Notrump. For example: if your RHO opened 2♡, an overcall of 4NT would be a good description holding this hand:
♠3 ♡6 ◇A K J 10 6 4 ♣K Q J 8 3.

What about an even better hand? From an online game I kibitzed, South held:
♠J ♡— ◇A K Q 9 8 6 ♣A K Q J 4 2. East opened 2♡. There were a variety of auctions, ranging from Blackwood (not very helpful), double, to 4NT, and others with most pairs reaching six of a minor.

A good agreement is that a jump cue bid – 4♡, in this case, over 2♡ – shows super minors, a hand too good for 4NT.

If North has: ♠A K 6 3 ♡Q 8 6 ◇5 4 3 ♣10 7 5, a grand might be reached:

West	North	East	South
		2♡	4♡
Pass	4♠*	Pass	7♣^
All Pass			

*Cue bid; partner asked for a minor

^ Pass or correct

UNUSUAL NOTRUMP PRACTICE DEALS

What's your bid after a 1♡ opening by RHO with each of the following hands:

(a) ♠4 ♡7 6 ◇Q J 10 5 4 ♣A Q J 9 2

(b) ♠K 5 ♡2 ◇K J 9 5 4 ♣Q 9 6 5 4

(c) ♠7 3 ♡2 ◇K Q J 9 6 ♣A K J 9 5

What's your bid after a 1♠ opening by RHO with each of the following hands:

(d) ♠A 4 ♡7 ◇A K 6 4 2 ♣A Q J 3 2

(e) ♠— ♡4 2 ◇Q 10 8 6 4 2 ♣K 9 8 6 5

(f) ♠5 4 ♡— ◇K J 9 7 5 ♣K Q 10 4 3 2

What's your bid after a 1♣ opening by RHO with this hand:

(g) ♠6 ♡K J 9 3 2 ◇A 10 5 4 3 2 ♣5

What's your bid after a 1◇ opening by RHO with this hand:

(h) ♠6 5 ♡K Q 10 9 3 ◇4 ♣K J 7 6 5

Answers

(a) 2NT at any vulnerability. A typical Unusual Notrump. Pass at the next opportunity unless forced.

(b) 2NT at favorable and equal vulnerability, then pass. A bit frisky at unfavorable with poor suit quality.

(c) 2NT at any vulnerability. The type previously treated as too good for this action.

(d) 2NT, then cue bid or splinter. Trying for slam if partner shows anything.

(e) 2NT at any vulnerability. The extra shape makes up for lack of values.

(f) 2NT, then raise 3♣ to 4♣. This shows good hand, but not like Hand (d).

(g) 2NT, any vulnerability. All the cards are working. Pass afterwards.

(h) 2NT at equal or favorable; 1♡ at unfavorable.

After the auction (1♢)–2NT–(Pass), what do you bid with:

(a) ♠ A Q 7 5 3 ♡ J 4 2 ♢ Q 3 2 ♣ 8 6?

After the auction (1♠)–2NT–(Pass), what do you bid with:

(b) ♠ K J 3 2 ♡ A 8 6 4 2 ♢ 10 2 ♣ 9 4?

After the auction (1♠)–2NT–(Pass), what do you bid with:

(c) ♠ 7 5 3 ♡ J 7 5 3 ♢ K 9 8 5 3 ♣ 2?

After the auction (1♣)–2NT–(Pass), what do you bid with:

(d) ♠ A J 6 4 ♡ K Q 3 ♢ 9 5 ♣ 9 8 4 2?

Answers

(a) 3♡. Choose between clubs and hearts, partner's suits.

(b) 3♣. With no clear preference, bid the lower suit, giving partner room. If RHO had bid, you would have passed.

(c) 5♢. Preempting against the opponents' likely 4♠.

(d) 3♣. Forcing, asking partner if he is weak or strong. If weak and no game interest, he bids 3♢, his lowest. If interested, he bids 3♡, his higher. If he bids 3♢, you bid 3♡. If he bids 3♡, you bid 4♡.

TRUST

At favorable vulnerability, South holds:

♠7 ♡3 ♢K Q 7 6 3 ♣K 10 8 6 5 2.

West	North	East	South
		1♠	2NT
Pass	3♣	3♡	Pass
4♡	Pass	Pass	?

The vulnerable opponents found their heart game. Do you want to sacrifice?

You have a little extra in the way of distribution. Your partner picked your longer suit. Are you jumping in the water? Do you think you can beat 4♡ ?
Do you think you can save for -500?

You have your first bid and little more. You made partner bid. He then passed over 4♡. He said 3♣ was high enough. Do you trust him?

The full deal:

West	North	East
	♠Q J 9 8 3	
	♡K 9 8 2	
	♢4 2	
	♣7 4	
♠4 2		♠A K 10 6 5
♡Q 5 4		♡A J 10 7 6
♢J 10 8 5		♢A 9
♣A Q 9 3		♣J
	♠7	
	♡3	
	♢K Q 7 6 3	
	♣K 10 8 6 5 2	

5♣ doubled is going to be expensive. Remember, you made North bid. If he had a fit with you, he would have done more than bid 3♣ the first time. If you trust his judgment, you can pass without a second thought.

TOUGH DECISION

With both side vulnerable, East holds:

♠Q J 10 4 3 ♡4 2 ◇A 9 2 ♣8 7 2.

West	North	East	South
			1♡
2NT	3♡	?	

Should East get involved? Is the 3–3 pattern in the suits West is showing enough to make some noise? You have some defense. Maybe South is passing? What to do? Bid or pass?

East passed, South bid game, and West led the ♣J:

West	North	East
	♠7 5 2	
	♡Q J 10 9	
	◇Q 7 6	
	♣Q 6 3	
♠6		♠Q J 10 4 3
♡8 3		♡4 2
◇K J 10 8 5		◇A 9 2
♣K J 10 9 5		♣8 7 2
	♠A K 9 8	
	♡A K 7 6 5	
	◇4 3	
	♣A 4	

Declarer won the opening lead with dummy's queen and lost two diamonds and a heart. East might have bid 4◇, not so much to suggest a save but to suggest an opening lead.

Declarer will then end up with a club loser as well.

FITS AND COVERS

With neither side vulnerable, East holds:

♠A 9 6 ♡9 7 5 ◊Q 9 6 2 ♣Q 7 5.

West	North	East	South
			1♡
2NT	3♡	?	

What, if anything, should East bid? At the table, East passed and South bid 4♡. N/S scored +420 when South took 10 tricks, losing one in each suit except hearts. What do you think of this result?

It's probably not very good. As East, you have a double fit in the minors. You also have one cover card, the ♠A, to park one of West's losers. How many tricks do you think your side would lose in 5◊? And what happens if they bid 5♡?

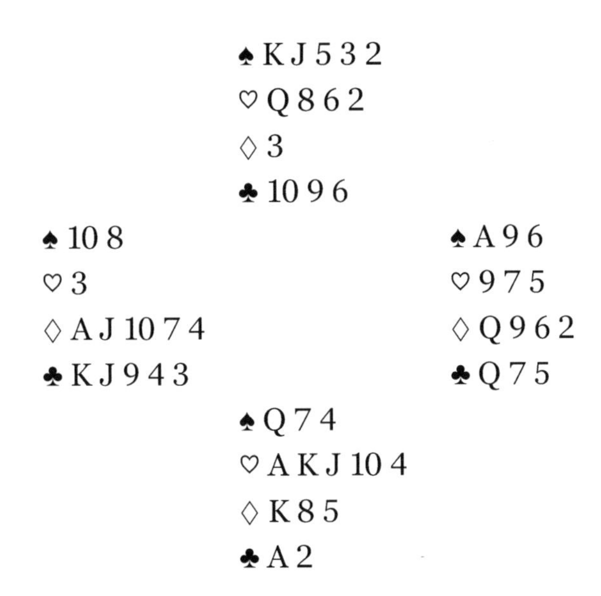

West	North / South	East
	♠K J 5 3 2 ♡Q 8 6 2 ◊3 ♣10 9 6	
♠10 8 ♡3 ◊A J 10 7 4 ♣K J 9 4 3		♠A 9 6 ♡9 7 5 ◊Q 9 6 2 ♣Q 7 5
	♠Q 7 4 ♡A K J 10 4 ◊K 8 5 ♣A 2	

Notice that in 5◊ doubled, E/W would be -300. And if N/S push on to 5♡, you would be +50.

Are you still satisfied with your -420?

UNUSUAL, BUT WITH IMPLICATIONS

North holds: ♠8 5 4 ♡K 6 5 4 3 2 ◇4 3 ♣J 9.

West	North	East	South
		1♠	2NT
4♠	Pass	Pass	4NT
?			

South must have a very good hand. 2NT was nothing special, minors, but now he is soloing to the five level.

What should North bid? Why?

Being 2–2 in the minors with better clubs, most would bid 5♣. But is that right? Think a little deeper. You know South has a lot of points, but what is her distribution?

If South had equal length in the minors, or more clubs, what would she probably have bid over 4♠? She would bid 5♣, no? So what does 4NT suggest?

Sure, longer diamonds. And you want to be in your longest trump suit. So North should bid 5◇, not 5♣.

South's hand: ♠ — ♡A 8 ◇A K 10 9 8 5 ♣A Q 10 7 2.

TWO LOWEST

Dlr: East Vul: N/S	♠A 8 4 3 ♡Q 5 3 ◇K 9 8 ♣K 9 5	
♠Q 10 5 2 ♡K 8 7 ◇5 4 ♣10 7 6 4		♠K J 7 6 ♡J 4 ◇Q 7 2 ♣A Q 8 3
	♠9 ♡A 10 9 6 2 ◇A J 10 6 3 ♣J 2	

West	North	East	South
		1♣	2NT
Pass	3♣	Pass	3◇
Pass	3♡	Pass	4♡
All Pass			

East opened 1♣ and South overcalled 2NT. The Unusual Notrump, while usually thought of as for the minors, can be used for the two lowest unbid suits, in this case, diamonds and hearts.

North has a three-card fit for both of South's suits and an outside ace. Interested in game, North cue bid 3♣. South, unsure where North was heading, bid 3◇.

North now bid 3♡, indicating she was interested in game in hearts, being too strong to have just bid hearts the first time.

With aces and reasonable spot cards, South bid 4♡

NOT HIGH ENOUGH

At unfavorable vul, East holds: ♠9 8 3 2 ♡10 6 ◊A 2 ♣A J 10 7 5.

West	North	East	South
			1◊
2NT	3◊	?	

I was West. The Unusual Notrump usually, but not always, shows the minors. It shows the two lowest unbid suits in this case, so after South opened 1◊, my 2NT showed clubs and hearts.

What should East bid? My student bravely bid 4♣. What a guy!

Do you agree or would you have done something else? The auction continued:

West	North	East	South
			1◊
2NT	3◊	4♣	4♠
?			

South who was on the way to 5◊, bid 4♠ just in case North had a spade fit.

I was in a no-win position. If I passed, I was -420. If I bid 5♣, I was minus 200. But if East had correctly bid not 4♣ but 5♣, South's choices were 5◊ going down or defending 5♣. The cold spade game would never have been discovered.

	North	
	♠J 10 6 5 ♡A J 3 2 ◊9 8 6 3 ♣4	
West		**East**
♠7 ♡K Q 9 8 5 ◊10 4 ♣K Q 8 6 2		♠9 8 3 2 ♡10 6 ◊A 2 ♣A J 10 7 5
	South	
	♠A K Q 4 ♡7 4 ◊K Q J 7 5 ♣9 3	

ODDS ON

With both sides vulnerable, South holds:

♠A 6 4 ♡6 ◊A 8 7 6 4 3 ♣K Q 7.

West	North	East	South
1♡	2NT	4♡	?

You are just finishing sorting your hand and counting all your high ones. You look up and already the bidding is at 4♡. That's just great!

So much for a scientific auction. What's it going to be? What are your choices?
4NT? What would that even mean?
5◊? Seems conservative.
5♡? Trying for seven? Playing partner for two aces? Seems unlikely.
6◊? Play partner for one ace? Reasonable, no?

The full deal:

	North	
	♠5	
	♡7 2	
	◊K J 10 9 2	
	♣A J 10 9 3	
♠K Q J 2		♠10 9 8 7 3
♡A Q J 8 5		♡K 10 9 4 3
◊Q		◊2
♣6 5 2		♣8 4
	♠A 6 4	
	♡6	
	◊A 8 7 6 4 3	
	♣K Q 7	

THE UNUSUAL 1NT

North holds: ♠A 9 7 6 2 ♡K 10 ♢Q 7 6 3 ♣10 2.

West	North	East	South
	Pass	Pass	Pass
1♡	Pass	1♠	1NT
2♡	?		

What does 1NT mean? One partner wanted to play that it showed a maximum passed hand. That is beyond terrible. Even if your partner were not a passed hand, why would you want to show some balanced 11-point hand?

1NT is take-out for the minors. Does South have to bid 2NT when 1NT can now do the job? Yes, South could double, but 1NT implies a more shapely hand. North should compete with 3♢. East takes the push to 3♡ and everyone passes:

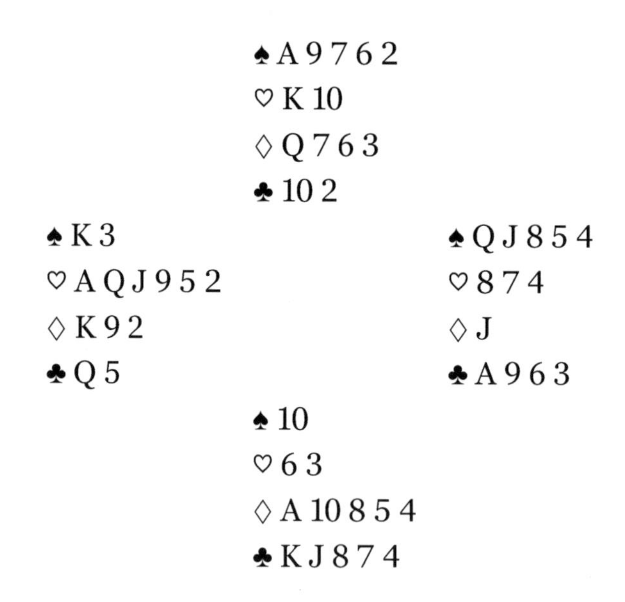

North:
♠A 9 7 6 2
♡K 10
♢Q 7 6 3
♣10 2

West:
♠K 3
♡A Q J 9 5 2
♢K 9 2
♣Q 5

East:
♠Q J 8 5 4
♡8 7 4
♢J
♣A 9 6 3

South:
♠10
♡6 3
♢A 10 8 5 4
♣K J 8 7 4

Note South did not bid over 3♡. He had his first bid but nothing extra. He has a chance to set 3♡. If North leads a club and declarer plays low, South will get a spade ruff.

A BIT OF A DELAY

North holds: ♠J 8 7 4 ♡A J 3 2 ◇ 10 9 6 4 ♣7.

West	North	East	South
		1♠	2♣
2♠	Pass	Pass	2NT
Pass	?		

North thought for awhile and passed. Do you think that is the right call? What's going on? What does South's 2NT bid suggest? So many questions.

South does not want to let the opponents play in their comfort zone, two of a major, and is balancing. Balancing with what?

2NT is the Delayed Unusual Notrump. South has both minors but longer, much longer clubs. But rather than bidding 3♣, he can introduce diamonds. If he had equal or close to equal length, he could have either started with 2NT, or started by bidding diamonds, then clubs.

North should bid 3◇. Whatever happens after that, N/S have pushed E/W higher or N/S will play in 3◇.

West	North	East
	♠J 8 7 4 ♡A J 3 2 ◇ 10 9 6 4 ♣7	
♠K 10 2 ♡Q 8 7 6 ◇Q 7 2 ♣Q 8 4		♠A Q 9 6 5 ♡K 10 9 ◇5 3 ♣K 6 2
	♠3 ♡5 4 ◇A K J 8 ♣A J 10 9 5 3	

This sequence often occurs at the four level. Suppose West, with a different hand, had bid 4♠. Now 4NT by South would be the same: both minors with much longer clubs.

WHAT'S GOING ON?

West holds: ♠K Q 10 7 4 ♡Q 10 9 ♢A 9 ♣Q 10 8

West	North	East	South
1♠	Dbl	Pass	2♡
Pass	Pass	2NT	Pass
?			

"Now what's she doing?" ponders West to himself. "Suddenly she found some high cards? Can this be natural?" What do you think?

East is balancing with a delayed Unusual Notrump. The opponents have stopped in their comfort zone, the two level. They likely have an eight-card fit. East has a smattering of high cards and wants to give them a push. East could bid 2♠ and play the 5–2 fit. East could risk 3♣, but partner might have diamonds.

The solution? 2NT. This can't be natural. West should be able to tell just from looking at his own hand. This must be two-suited, showing clubs and diamonds. Bid 3♣.

West	North	East
	♠5 3 ♡A K 8 7 ♢Q 7 4 3 ♣A 6 2	
♠K Q 10 7 4 ♡Q 10 9 ♢A 9 ♣Q 10 8		♠A 6 ♡J 3 ♢K 8 5 2 ♣J 9 7 5 3
	♠J 9 8 2 ♡6 5 4 2 ♢J 10 6 ♣K 4	

2NT in the Fourth Seat

North

♠ 9 4

♡ 10 6 5 3

◇ J 6

♣ A 8 7 4 2

West	North	East	South
1♠	P	P	2NT
P	?		

What should North bid? What does South's 2NT bid mean? Is it unusual for the minors?

The Unusual 2NT is good for interfering with the opponents but on this auction, the cat is out of the bag. West knows East is weak. There is no need for 2NT in the balancing seat to be Unusual.

1NT shows 12 to 15+ and double followed by notrump shows 16 – 18+. This 2NT shows more, in the 19 – 20 range.

South's hand: ♠ Q J 8 6 ♡ A K ◇ A 10 7 5 ♣ K Q 10

CHAPTER 5

Ghestem and CRO

GHESTEM, A POPULAR TWO-SUITED CONVENTION

Ghestem was invented by the French bridge and checkers player, Pierre Ghestem. It has the same basic requirements as Michaels, but the meanings of the bids differ in that they are more specific than Michaels.

The general principle, as we shall see, is that, except for (1♣)–2♣ being natural, jump overcalls show the three possible two-suited hands excluding the opened suit using this format:

2NT shows the two lowest unbid suits
3♣ shows the two highest ranked unbid suits
A cue bid shows the top- and bottom-ranking unbid suits

Therefore, we have this:

After RHO opens 1♣:
2♣ = natural, clubs
2♢ = the two unbid suits, hearts and spades
2NT = the two lowest unbid suits, diamonds and hearts
3♣ = the two "extreme" suits, diamonds and spades

After RHO opens 1♢:
2♢ = the top and bottom suits, clubs and spades
2NT = the two lowest unbid suits, clubs and hearts
3♣ = the two highest unbid suits, hearts and spades

After RHO opens 1♡:
2♡ = the top and bottom suits, clubs and spades
2NT = the two lowest unbid suits, clubs and diamonds
3♣ = the two highest unbid suits, diamonds and spades

After RHO opens 1♠:
2♠ = the top and bottom suits, clubs and hearts
2NT = the two lowest unbid suits, clubs and diamonds
3♣ = the two highest unbid suits, diamonds and hearts

COMPARISON OF MICHAELS TO GHESTEM

Ghestem is more precise in terms of defining the specific suits noted. On some auctions, the responder to the Michaels bid does not know both of her partner's suits. This may inhibit preemptive action early in the auction. The Michaels Cue Bid used in combination with the Unusual Notrump does not cater for a two-suiter in spades and the other minor. The overcaller probably simply starts by just bidding spades.

However, Ghestem has the disadvantage that you cannot choose a major at the two level. These obstacles are overcome by the different variations on the systems as we have described, such as the Questem variant of Ghestem.

It is best to play Ghestem as showing a wide range of values. The beauty of the convention is partner knows your precise distribution and can judge what to bid.

Many feel this is the better of the two-suited overcall systems. Granted, you lose your natural 3♣ jump overcall. If you feel this is too serious a loss, then Ghestem is not for you. Like any convention, one has to usually give up something to use something else. Likewise, there is a bit more memorization involved than playing Michaels. If this is a strain on you or your partner, you need decide which to play.

However, the advantage is partner knows your suits immediately and should strive to bid to the level of the fit. Weak, strong, or in-between, when you have a known fit, try to bid aggressively. Whether you make what you bid is not the point.

If you have a fit, the likelihood is the opponents have one too. At the same time, you need be conservative with misfitting hands.

The disadvantages are two-fold. As mentioned, one is the loss of the natural 3♣ overcall. The other is by using 3♣ over an opposing minor-suit opening to denote both majors, the majors cannot be bid at the two level as in Michaels.

GHESTEM VARIATIONS

A modified structure to retain the 3♣ overcall is this one after RHO opens 1♢:

2NT = the two lowest unbid suits

2♢ = the top and bottom suits, i.e., clubs and spades

3♣ = natural

3♢ = majors

To overcome the problem of introducing the majors at the three-level after 1♣:

2♣ = natural

2♢ = majors

2♡/2♠ = natural

2NT = the two lowest suits, diamonds and hearts

3♣ = the pointed suits, diamonds and spades

Another variation to allow introduction of the majors at the two level, attributed to Benito Garozzo, follows. After RHO opens one of a minor:

2♣ = natural

2♢ = majors

2NT = the two lowest unbid suits

3♣ = top and bottom suits over 1♢, non-forcing

In this variation, you have the ability to make a natural 2♣ overcall, especially useful over artificial or short club openings.

As (1♢)–3♣ is non-forcing, many partnerships playing Ghestem ala Garozzo use (1♢)–3♢ to indicate a very strong, black, two-suited hand.

Inverted Ghestem: Questem

Another variation to avoid the problem of starting the majors at the three level is to simply "invert" the cue bid and the 3♣ bid. For want of a better name, we have Questem:

Direct cue bid = the two highest suits

2NT = the two lowest suits

3♣ = the highest and lowest suits

CRO: ANOTHER TWO-SUITED CONVENTION

While Michaels and the Unusual Notrump are the two most common two-suited conventions, there are others. For example, there's CRO, an initialism that stands for Color, Rank, Odd:

After RHO opens 1♣:	2♣ = ♢ & ♡, Color (red)
	2NT = ♡ & ♠, Rank (majors)
	3♣ = ♢ & ♠, Odd
After RHO opens 1♢:	2♢ = ♣ & ♠, Color (black)
	2NT = ♡ & ♠, Rank (majors)
	3♣ = ♣ & ♡, Odd
After RHO opens 1♡:	2♡ = ♣ & ♠, Color (black)
	2NT = ♣ & ♢, Rank (minors)
	3♣ = ♢ & ♠, Odd
After RHO opens 1♠:	2♠ = ♢ & ♡, Color (red)
	2NT = ♣ & ♢, Rank (minors)
	3♣ = ♣ & ♡, Odd

The advantage of CRO is that partner knows your exact two suits. The disadvantage is being forced to the three level after (1 minor)–2 minor.

Also, the 3♣ preemptive bid is no longer available. Like the other conventions, this is used with weak and strong hands.

CHAPTER 6

Defense Against Two-Suited Overcalls

DEFENSE AGAINST TWO-SUITED OVERCALLS

The purpose of a defense is to allow responder to (1) distinguish between strong and competitive hands in the two suits not promised by the overcaller, and (2) to distinguish various raises of opener's suit if he has support.

There are variations to this defense. Sometimes it's called Unusual versus Unusual, and also Incredible versus Unusual. But the less to memorize, the less to forget. It's important to keep a system logical and uniform. I suggest the following "basic" approach:

We open and the next hand shows a two-suiter (*which* suits don't matter)

When both suits are known:

(a) The lower cue bid is non-forcing in the fourth suit.

(b) The higher cue bid is a limit raise or better in opener's suit.

This is generic; it doesn't matter what the suit(s) are. You will read other defenses that vary with the opening bids; high/high, low/low, etc., that I believe are much more confusing and require more memorization.

**See addendum at end of this chapter (Extended Defense).

You decide, but I urge you to look how simple above (a) and (b) are

You open 1♠, LHO overcalls 2NT (minors). Partner bids:

3♣ = Non-forcing in hearts, the fourth suit
3♢ = Limit raise or better in spades
3♡ = Natural, forcing
3♠ = Competitive raise
4 Minor = Splinter raise in spades

You open 1♡, LHO overcalls 2NT (minors). Partner bids:

3♣ = Non-forcing in spades, the fourth suit
3♢ = Limit raise or better in hearts
3♡ = Competitive raise
3♠ = Natural, forcing
4 Minor = Splinter raise in hearts

You open 1◊, LHO overcalls 2◊ (majors). Partner bids:

2♡ = Non-forcing clubs, the fourth suit

2♠ = Limit raise or better in diamonds

2NT = Natural, invitational

3♣ = Natural, forcing

3◊ = Competitive raise

3 Major = Splinter raise in diamonds

Note that after 1♣–(2♣): 2◊ is non-forcing (no need to use 2♡ for that), so 2♡ is forcing in diamonds, and 2♠ is a limit raise or better in clubs.

Notice there is nothing to think about other than the two generic guidelines.

What about pass and double? Pass is either neutral or a desire to penalize BOTH of their suits. Double is a desire to penalize ONE of the suits without shortness in the other. Be sure to discuss this with your partner. See the fifth example below.

Let's try a few example hands: The auction has proceeded 1♠ by partner and 2NT (clubs and diamonds) on your right.

♠J 9 7 5 ♡A 7 5 3 ◊5 ♣8 6 4 2

Bid 3♠. A competitive raise. Yes, the three level may feel too high, but you have four trumps and a singleton; partner won't be too unhappy. Support with support.

♠K J 5 3 ♡A Q 5 4 ◊7 5 3 ♣8 7

Bid 3◊. The higher cue bid shows a limit raise or better in partner's suit. A minimum, but all your cards are working.

♠9 6 ♡A Q 7 5 4 ◊K 8 7 6 ♣A J

Bid 3♡, natural and forcing. (With less than a game force, bid 3♣ instead.)

♠4 3 ♡K Q 10 6 4 2 ◊9 4 3 ♣K 8

Bid 3♣, which is non-forcing in the "fourth" suit, hearts here. Compare to the previous example.

♠2 ♡J 8 6 4 ◊K J 8 4 ♣A J 7 4

Pass ... and then double for penalty. Your LHO has to bid.

♠K 10 5 3 2 ♡A J 5 ◊A 8 4 2 ♣2

Bid 4♣, a splinter raise to at least game.

We open and the next hand shows a two-suiter (*which* suits don't matter)

When only one suit is known:

(a) A cue bid is a limit raise or better in opener's suit

(b) New suits are natural and forcing

You open 1♠, LHO overcalls 2♠ (hearts and a minor). Partner bids:

3♣ = Natural, forcing

3♢ = Natural, forcing

3♡ = Limit raise or better in spades

3♠ = Competitive raise

This all sounds simple, but, of course, hands will come up that don't fit into any of the above descriptions, such as hands with ten or more HCP, lacking support for opener's suit. The trickiest auctions are those where you have game-forcing strength without clear direction and without sure stoppers in all unbid suits.

In these cases, your most likely target game is 3NT, but with one of the overcaller's suits unknown, the search for stoppers is not an exact science. The best strategy is usually to start with double. Then, with more information and partner's action, you will have a better idea of how to proceed.

If partner has a hand unsuitable for defending such as a near-solid trump suit of at least six cards or a strong two-suiter, he may show it.

After your initial double, you are in a forcing situation. Assuming partner passes and the bidding comes back to you, a subsequent double is penalty. Passing over RHO's rebid is forcing, suggesting a tolerance for defending.

A new suit is game forcing. A delayed cue bid of overcaller's major is game forcing, denies a stopper in the suit the opponents have chosen, and asks partner to bid 3NT if she can.

USING SOME JUDGMENT

These agreements will handle most of your problems, but you will need judgment. It sounds easy on paper, but at the table, I can tell you it just isn't so simple. To declare or defend is often the question after these overcalls. Here are some suggestions.

Probable bad breaks are on the horizon. Suits are not splitting. If it's going to be close, close games may be doomed, especially with only an eight-card trump fit.

The best time to compete is when you have a trump fit. The number of trumps far outweighs high-card strength. If you have four or more trumps, stretch to compete. Only three? Stay conservative.

Plan ahead. Consider your next bid before deciding to double or make a cue bid. What further bids will be available?

Scattered values without a fit suggest defending. Even with three-card trump support, if your strength is in the opponent's suits, a big juicy penalty may be waiting. The vulnerability is important, but even at equal, taking a sure plus score is often best.

Lead a trump against a doubled contract.

Let's look at some problem hands after partner opens 1♠ and your RHO bids 2♠, hearts and a minor:

♠Q 7 ♡A J 9 4 ◇5 2 ♣A Q 9 7 5
Double. It's unlikely the opponents will end up in hearts. More likely, they will reach 3◇. Your 3♡ cue bid then asks partner to bid 3NT with a diamond stopper.

♠J 3 ♡A 9 7 ◇K J 4 2 ♣Q 10 5 3
Double. Defending will likely be your best score at any vulnerability except unfavorable. Even then, I'd take the plus score. No? OK, bid 2NT and let them off the hook. Are you playing against a relative?

♠J 6 3 ♡Q 3 2 ♢K J 6 ♣K 8 7 6

3♠. I'd make a single raise. The 3=3=3=4 shape with queens and jacks is not a limit raise in my book. Close.

♠10 9 6 4 ♡2 ♢A 10 6 4 ♣9 7 5 3

3♠. I know, the three level with this? But you have four trumps and a singleton. Another trump, it's almost a 4♠ bid.

♠K J 10 2 ♡6 4 ♢J 2 ♣A 9 7 5 3

3♡. Yes, cue bid to show a limit raise. It's only 9 HCP, but compare this to the third example with 10 HCP where we only made a single raise. Which hand do you think partner will prefer?

♠6 4 ♡A 10 ♢A K Q 10 3 2 ♣J 5 2

3NT. Before anyone knows who has what. LHO has to guess the lead. A good partner has a club stopper.

EXTENDED DEFENSE FOR TWO-SUITED OVERCALLS AFTER 1M

If you want to add a tiny bit, think about this. These auctions often get competitive and high-level decisions are needed. By the time the bidding comes back to the opening bidder, it's often at the four or five level.

What to do? Pass? Bid five? Double? How good is my partner's hand who made that limit raise or better? How much better?

One easy addition to everything on the previous page will help. Notice 3NT was not an option. In all the major openings, if the opponents bid Michaels or the Unusual Notrump, change the higher cue bid to exactly a limit raise, not "or better." This will help opener know what to do later.

Simply add 3NT as an artificial game-forcing raise in all those auctions. If opener knows you only had a limit raise, the five level is probably too high.
An example:

West	North	East	South
1♠	2NT	?	

3♢ = Limit raise in spades
3NT = Forcing raise in spades

If South bids 5♣ or 5♢ – not a big surprise – West will have more information if deciding between declaring or defending.

** Addendum: You will read elsewhere that some prefer playing the reverse; that after 1 Major is overcalled with a 2-suited bid, the lower cue bid is a limit raise or better and the higher cue bid is forcing in the fourth suit. Or the reverse, and bidding the fourth suit is non-forcing. Sometimes this is called 'lower-lower' or other names. I find generic to be much easier.

And if partner opens 1♡ and the next hand bids 2NT, if your 3♠ bid is non-forcing, how do we stop in 3♡?

CHAPTER 7

Miscellaneous Competitive Auctions

MISCELLANEOUS COMPETITIVE AUCTIONS

Most of the guidelines we have discussed are straightforward and not difficult to follow. But understanding basic underlying principles is more important than trying to memorize "rules."

Often the opposition will interfere. A common-sense approach based on having a good understanding of the underlying principles is required. Yes, some basics we memorize, but for the rest, you will often find yourself in uncharted territory.

We did discuss when the opponents use Michaels and the Unusual Notrump after we open the bidding. Those few basic principles are easy to learn.

It's a bit ironic that when we are doing the preempting, it's a little more playing by feel.

The following deals may help to illustrate these principles.

PASS, BID, OR DOUBLE?

South holds: ♠ 6 4 ♡ J 6 2 ◇ A 10 8 5 ♣ 10 9 4 2.

West	North	East	South
	1◇	2◇	?

Partner opens 1◇ and your RHO bids 2◇, a Michaels Cue Bid for the majors. Do you want to get involved? Your options include pass, double, or 3◇. Which do you prefer?

3◇ should show about 10 support points, maybe a tad less.

What about double? If you had a natural bid, you would have made it. Double says you have 10+ points and no convenient bid. But you are showing values AND you promise one more bid.

You should play that double is forcing to 2NT or three of your suit — or you double the opponents.

This means if you double, you cannot pass out the opponents in 2♡ or 2♠. At the three level, you would be allowed to pass.

Therefore, with South's meager values, pass is the best option.

BID OR DOUBLE?

Dlr: South
Vul: N/S

North:
♠ A J 6 5
♡ 10 8 7 6 4
♢ A Q
♣ 6 4

West:
♠ 4
♡ K Q J 9 5
♢ 6 4
♣ A 10 9 7 3

East:
♠ 10 9 2
♡ 2
♢ J 9 8 5 3
♣ Q J 8 2

South:
♠ K Q 8 7 3
♡ A 3
♢ K 10 7 2
♣ K 5

West	North	East	South
			1♠
2♠	3♡	4NT	Pass
5♣	Pass	Pass	Dbl
All Pass			

A Michaels Cue Bid of a major requires a better hand than that of a minor, especially the above auction. The bidding is being rapidly pushed to the three level with one suit unknown. There are often difficulties sorting out who has what and who can make what.

North's 3♡ cue bid showed exactly a limit raise. As we discussed, it's often important for responder to differentiate between a limit raise and a game-forcing raise, because opener is often faced with a five-level decision.

Take South's problem in the above deal: Should he bid 5♠ or take whatever plus score he can get by defending 5♣ doubled? Here, South knew his partner had only a limit raise, so he took the plus score, +300.

But North-South can score +620 and probable +650. It's easy sitting here, but not so easy at the table.

SPLINTERS AFTER THEIR MICHAELS

South holds: ♠8 ♡6 3 ◇K J 7 4 3 ♣A Q 9 7 5.

West	North	East	South
	1◇	2◇	?

Your partner opens 1◇ and RHO bids 2◇, a Michaels Cue Bid for the majors.

What should you do? What are your choices?

You might make a negative double, which would show values and presumably the other suits. But the most descriptive bid is 3♠. This is a splinter bid showing shortness, game-forcing values and diamond support.

You must have done something right, because after your 3♠, partner asks for keycards. How to do so is another topic, but you have two keycards without the queen. I do not think you have enough 'extra' length to make up for the queen. Partner bids 6◇:

	North	
	♠10 7 2	
	♡A J 8	
	◇A Q 8 6 2	
	♣K 8	
West		**East**
♠Q 9 4 3		♠A K J 6 5
♡K 7 5		♡Q 10 9 4 2
◇9 5		◇10
♣J 6 3 2		♣10 4
	South	
	♠8	
	♡6 3	
	◇K J 7 4 3	
	♣A Q 9 7 5	

6◇ is a good slam as long as clubs are no worse than 4–2.

CREATING A FORCE

With both sides vulnerable, South holds: ♠8 ♡Q 7 6 ◊A Q J 6 5 2 ♣A J 8.

West	North	East	South
	1♣	2♣	2◊
3♠	Pass	Pass	4◊
All Pass			

Here's the full deal:

	♠A 7 3 ♡K J 8 ◊10 7 4 ♣K Q 9 2	
♠Q 9 5 4 ♡10 5 ◊K 8 ♣10 7 6 5 4		♠K J 10 6 2 ♡A 9 4 3 2 ◊9 3 ♣3
	♠8 ♡Q 7 6 ◊A Q J 6 5 2 ♣A J 8	

Do you agree with South's bidding? Even though North's hand was a flat 13-count with three small diamonds, 6◊ was on a finesse. Who was to blame for not even reaching game?

100% South. Was 2◊ forcing? NO! 2♡ is forcing in diamonds. After Michaels, 2◊ shows five or six diamonds and 8–10 HCP. 3◊ would show more diamonds but still would be non-forcing. So the above auction was non-forcing, and North had a minimum.

What could South have bid? Double first and then bid diamonds. Double promises another bid, remember? After starting with double, South can bid 4◊ and North will bid 5◊. A difficult sequence, but North will know from South's failure to bid 2◊ or 3◊ diamonds earlier, that this sequence is forcing.

ON THE OTHER HAND

South holds: ♠K 7 6 ♡3 2 ◇K Q 10 8 5 ♣6 5 4.

West	North	East	South
	1♣	2♣	?

North opens, and East bids Michaels for the majors. What can South do? Does she have enough values to bid 2◇? Would that be the same as a 2/1 in competition, normally close to, but not always a game-forcing bid?

When the opponents bid Michaels, the bidding can often get out of hand. Everyone often is about to start jumping around. You may never get another chance to bid. After Michaels, most treat a bid in the unbid minor as non-forcing.

To force, you need to start with double or 2♡. So South has plenty to bid 2◇ in this case.

West	North	East	South
	1♣	2♣	2◇
2♠	3◇	All Pass	

	North	
	♠J 9 ♡A 9 7 5 ◇A J 6 ♣K J 10 9	
West ♠Q 8 2 ♡Q 8 ◇9 4 3 2 ♣A 7 3 2		**East** ♠A 10 5 4 3 ♡K J 10 6 4 ◇7 ♣Q 8
	♠K 7 6 ♡3 2 ◇K Q 10 8 5 ♣6 5 4	

Reaching 3◇ was good; it may or may not make. But the opponents were in 2♠ which was making. Without this agreement, South would not have bid.

AND FINALLY

South holds: ♠K 6 ♡5 2 ◇K Q J 9 6 5 ♣9 4 3.

West	North	East	South
	1♣	2♣	?

Partner opens and, once again, pesky East bids Michaels. I guess he has no other bids in his bidding box. What should South do? South is certainly bidding, but what?

We have seen some similar problems on the previous two deals. To review some understandings:

2◇ = Five or six diamonds, 8–10 HCP
3◇ = Six or seven diamonds, 9–11 HCP

And after 1◇–2◇:

3♣ = Six or seven clubs, 9–11 HCP

All these are non-forcing, an attempt to show your hand before the bidding goes wild.

South should bid 3◇. On this deal, everyone passes. That sounds ominous.

	North	
	♠A Q 5 4	
	♡K J 8 7	
	◇4	
	♣Q 10 6 5	
♠7 3		♠J 10 9 8 2
♡Q 6		♡A 10 9 4 3
◇10 7 3 2		◇A 8
♣K J 8 7 2		♣A
	♠K 6	
	♡5 2	
	◇K Q J 9 6 5	
	♣9 4 3	

N/S were probably going down on any auction and certainly not making 3NT.

KEEP SWINGING THE BAT

With E/W vulnerable, South holds: ♠Q 10 7 3 ♡Q 8 4 ♢K J 9 7 ♣K 6.

West	North	East	South
	1♣	2♣	?

What should South's first call be? South has an invitational hand. The choices seem to be 2♠, 2NT or double. Your side has the balance of power. Double is reasonable. It says you have a good hand without direction. No other call right now is appealing, AND you promise to bid again. The auction continues:

West	North	East	South
	1♣	2♣	Dbl
2♡	Pass	Pass	?

OK, your turn again. Now what? If they had bid spades, you would have had an easy double. Partner passed. Declarer or defend? 2NT? Maybe if the opponents were not vulnerable. If you cannot make game, maybe you should defend? So double again.

	North	
	♠5 2	
	♡K 5	
	♢A 6 5 3	
	♣A J 8 7 4	
♠K 4		♠A J 9 8 6
♡10 9 3		♡A J 7 6 2
♢10 8 2		♢Q 4
♣Q 10 9 5 3		♣2
	♠Q 10 7 3	
	♡Q 8 4	
	♢K J 9 7	
	♣K 6	

2♡ doubled is down at least one with a trump lead. It's important to understand what your bids mean after the opponents bid Michaels or any other convention.

A COMPETITIVE BATTLE

With both sides vul, South holds: ♠K J 10 ♡A Q 6 2 ◇ 10 8 7 5 4 ♣5.

West	North	East	South
		1◇	Pass
1♠	2NT	3♠	?

What should South do? Does North have a big hand? The minors? What?

The Unusual Notrump comes in all shapes and sizes. North is showing the two unbid suits, hearts and clubs. He does not have a strong hand in high cards or he would have made a take-out double. His bid is based more on distribution.

South has a great hand in support with four hearts to the A–Q and a singleton. If partner has five hearts to the king and an outside ace, game in hearts should be cold.

When you bid 4♡, West carries on to 4♠. This is passed back to you. Now what?

I think you should double. You have two sure tricks, and three if East has the ♠Q. If partner has nothing more than the ◇A, 4♠ is down:

	North	
	♠3 ♡K J 10 7 5 ◇2 ♣K J 10 4 3 2	
West ♠A 8 7 6 2 ♡4 ◇K 9 6 ♣Q 9 7 6		**East** ♠Q 9 5 4 ♡9 8 3 ◇A Q J 3 ♣A 8
	♠K J 10 ♡A Q 6 2 ◇10 8 7 5 4 ♣5	
	South	

AFTER A MICHAELS CUE BID

	♠A 10 6 ♡10 6 5 ♢K 9 ♣A Q 8 4 3	
♠K 8 3 ♡J 9 4 3 ♢J 7 5 2 ♣9 5		♠Q J 9 7 5 ♡A K Q 8 2 ♢10 3 ♣10
	♠4 2 ♡7 ♢A Q 8 6 4 ♣K J 7 6 2	

West	North	East	South
	1♣	2♣	3♡
Pass	4♢	Pass	4NT
Pass	6♣	All Pass	

2♣ showed the majors. 3♡ was a splinter showing clubs and short hearts. 4♢, by agreement, was a keycard ask in clubs, and 4NT showed 2 keycards with the ♣Q.

South had a good hand, and hoping North had more than three clubs, made a big club raise, showing heart shortness on the way.

North was looking at three small hearts. This pair was playing that the suit above the minor was the keycard asking bid, keeping the responses from going past 5♣.

When South showed two keycards, North could bid 6♣. A good slam, only needing diamonds to be no worse than 4–2.

SUPPORT

With E/W vul., South holds: ♠6 2 ♡A 5 3 ◇K J 7 5 2 ♣10 8 3.

West	North	East	South
	1◇	2◇	?

Should South double? No, a double would show 11 or so HCP and usually a hand with no clear bid. Here, you have support for partner, an easy raise. Bid 3◇.

West jumps to 4♡, and North carries on to 5◇. Saving? To make? Well, you have your bid.

West	North / South	East
	♠A K 9 3 ♡6 ◇A 10 6 4 3 ♣K 4 2	
♠8 5 ♡K 9 4 2 ◇Q 8 ♣Q J 9 7 5		♠Q J 10 7 4 ♡Q J 10 8 7 ◇9 ♣A 6
	♠6 2 ♡A 5 3 ◇K J 7 5 2 ♣10 8 3	

N/S have reached a good contract. Can North make 5◇ with the ♣A in East's hand?

After eliminating the hearts, North can play the ♠A K and ruff a spade. On the last spade, he can discard a club, a loser-on-loser play. East is endplayed. He has to give you a ruff/sluff or lead a club.

A HEADACHE

	♠10 7 5 ♡A 4 ♢9 8 4 2 ♣8 4 3 2	
♠K 8 3 ♡8 7 3 ♢K J 10 ♣K Q J 6		♠Q 6 ♡Q 10 6 ♢A Q 6 3 ♣A 10 9 5
	♠A J 9 4 2 ♡K J 9 5 2 ♢7 5 ♣7	

West	North	East	South
		1♢	2♢
?			

East opened 1♢, and South bid 2♢ showing the majors. What should West do? What are his choices?

He has an opening hand. Double seems reasonable but may be just postponing his problem. Bid 2♠, his fragment? He can't want to play in one of South's suits. Bid 3♣? That's certainly an underbid with an opening hand facing an opening hand. 3NT and hope? Houston, we have a problem.

East–West will have to fend for themselves. They might have been in trouble anyhow. They can make 3♣. 3NT is doomed with a spade lead. And North–South can make a few spades.

Anyhow, it's not my problem. I just write this stuff; I don't have to have all the answers!

SEARCHING

With none vulnerable, South holds: ♠7 3 ♡A K J ◊Q 8 6 2 ♣K 6 5 2.

West	North	East	South
	1♣	2♣	?

North opened the bidding, and South has an opening hand. How should he proceed after East's Michaels Cue Bid? What are his choices?

3♣? Too strong. 4♣? Gives up on 3NT. Double? Then what? Other options?

The most likely contract will be 3NT if North has a spade stopper. So South starts by bidding 2♡, forcing for at least one round and obviously showing a fragment stopper. The auction continues:

West	North	East	South
	1♣	2♣	2♡
2♠	Pass	Pass	?

Now what? South is worth another bid. Try 3♡. Now partner at least knows you have game-forcing values. If he can bid 3NT, he will.

North continues with 4♣, no spade stopper. Now what? Are you getting tired of this question? 5♣ it is. You don't have to play it:

West	North	East
	♠Q 4	
	♡10 7 2	
	◊A J 9	
	♣A Q 10 9 8	
♠J 10 8 2		♠A K 9 6 5
♡9 6		♡Q 8 5 4 3
◊K 10 7 5 4		◊3
♣J 3		♣7 4
	♠7 3	
	♡A K J	
	◊Q 8 6 2	
	♣K 6 5 2	

North will make 5♣ if he guesses the diamond layout. East may lead his singleton diamond. Be sure to say "Good luck, partner."

STILL SEARCHING

With none vulnerable, South holds: ♠K Q 9 ♡7 6 ◇A J 8 6 2 ♣J 10 4.

West	North	East	South
	1♣	2♣	?

An invitational hand. 2◇? Double? Other? How about bidding our fragment again, 2♠, trying to reach 3NT? A reasonable choice.

Partner bids 2NT. Now what?

I think you should pass. You told partner you had some values, but you have a minimum. If North had extras, he would have bid 3NT, 2NT being non-forcing.

	North	
	♠8 7 ♡Q J 8 3 ◇Q 9 4 ♣A K 8 2	
West ♠6 3 2 ♡5 4 ◇K 10 7 3 ♣Q 6 5 3		**East** ♠A J 10 5 4 ♡A K 10 9 2 ◇5 ♣9 7
	♠K Q 9 ♡7 6 ◇A J 8 6 2 ♣J 10 4	

A reasonable auction to a contract that may or may not succeed.